HEARTS of CHAMPIONS

MARK TODD

HEARTS OF CHAMPIONS

Mark Todd, Hearts of Champions

ISBN 1-887002-66-9

Cross Training Publishing
P.O. Box 1541
Grand Island, NE 68802
(308) 384-5762

Library of Congress Cataloging in Publication Data in Progress.

Published by Cross Training Publishing,
P.O. Box 1541
Grand Island, NE 68802
1-800-430-8588

Photo Credit:
University of Nebraska Sports Information
Seattle Seahawks Public Relations - page 73
Atlanta Falcons Public Relations - page 91

ACKNOWLEDGEMENTS

The individuals and teams associated with the success of the Nebraska football program deserve the honor and recognition that they receive. Yet those moments of glory will continue to be fleeting. Coaches and players, no matter how successful, will constantly have their victories judged by a standard that reads, "What have you done for me lately?" And though it may not be a just measuring stick, it remains symbolic of how every victory eventually fades in its brilliance.

The tragic death of 22-year old Nebraska quarterback Brook Berringer in a plane crash on April 18, 1996 truly illuminates the things in life that are most important—an individual's relationship with and character reflective of the Lord God of the universe.

The late Berringer's teammate, free safety Tony Veland summarized things well following that tragic incident.

"Brook won the biggest championship of his life when he committed himself to the Lord," the defensive captain said. "And that's where he's at right now. He's in a far better place than he ever would have been here. So, although we mourn, we rejoice for him."

This book is dedicated in memory of Brook Berringer and has been written to present the impact of Jesus Christ on the lives of selected individuals involved with the Cornhusker football program. Though these men are imperfect, and this book does not include a complete list of outstanding players and coaches, it is my desire that their testimonies will provide hope and direction to anyone reading this publication.

I would like to extend a big "thank you" to the University of Nebraska Sports Information staff for their help in providing the necessary data and photographs for this project. Each of your efforts are greatly appreciated. Thank you coaches and former Husker players who were involved with this project. This book would not have been possible without your participation. Also, thanks Dad, Mom, Dan, friends and family for the inspiration.

Sincerely,

Mark Todd

FOREWORD

All I ever wanted to do was play football for the Nebraska Cornhuskers, while I was growing up in Lincoln. And when I finally got my chance back in the late 1970s, I discovered there was more to life than football. Each of the players and coaches included in this book came to that same conclusion. This book chronicles many of the greatest Nebraska players and coaches during the past three decades. Each of them have demonstrated a winning attitude in football and life.

No doubt, there are many more players and coaches associated with the Nebraska program that could be included in this book if length permitted. But I'm sure you'll be encouraged and inspired by each of these stories about faith, football, and family. Though Mark Todd never scored a touchdown for the Huskers on the field, he has definitely given every fan something to cheer about with *Hearts of Champions*.

Sincerely,

Gordon Thiessen
Publisher
Nebraska Defensive End, 1975-1980

Contents

The Coaches
Business As Usual

Continuity has been a key in building a successful tradition in the Husker program. The stay of the Nebraska assistant coach has averaged over a dozen years. The football program has only known two different head coaches since 1962.

The late Bob Devaney jumped-started the Nebraska football program in the early 1960s and established a standard of excellence with back-to-back national championships in 1970-71. The 1971 team has stood as one of the best of all time.

Formerly a full-time assistant under Devaney, Head Coach Tom Osborne has carried on the tradition of success since 1973 with annual bowl appearances, at least nine wins each season, and two national titles. Teamwork and integrity has described Osborne and the assistants with whom he has surrounded himself.

A closer look into the lives of several of these coaches reveals their basis for that commitment to excellence.

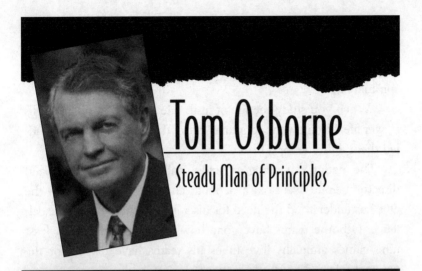

Tom Osborne
Steady Man of Principles

Head Coach
1973-present

It has not changed him. Whether triumph or tragedy, the solemn, yet serene, gentleman football coach of the plains has remained committed to his principles. Consistency has trademarked his personal and professional life. The quiet steadiness and perseverance of Tom Osborne can be traced to a foundation of faith in God.

"There has to be a steady, regular dimension to your faith," Osborne said. "Faith is not very effective if it's only practiced in a crisis. When you're really up against it, sometimes it's very easy to get very spiritual. And, yet, there's no real power, there's no real strength in that."

Osborne likened one with a stagnant faith to a would-be weight lifter who spends little time in the gym.

"It would be somewhat like if you wanted to be a 300-pound bench presser. If the only time you went into the weight room was Christmas and Easter, you're not going to get 300 pounds up, you're not even going to get 100 pounds up.

"Consider if discipline is critical in athletics—and there are certain things that you have to do with absolute precision, and you do them over and over again. And I think it's the same way in our spiritual life.

"When you study the life of Jesus, He was very regular in His prayer life. He knew the scriptures better than the people who studied them full-time for a living."

The nation's winningest active college football coach and director behind Nebraska's national championship teams of the '90s has understood the need for discipline in the pursuit of excellence. Osborne teams have gone bowling and have won at least nine games annually. Five times his teams have played for the national title and have won it twice.

It's been said that, "Winning is not everything." For Osborne, life is an endurance race. A consistent commitment to honoring God is vital. The process of character development within that pilgrimage bears a greater value than external success.

"All I can try to do is to be consistent and be faithful, then hopefully, that might bear some positive fruit.

"I live in a very unstable world of athletics where if you base your security on the won-loss record or the job that you have or whatever, you're certainly in a roller coaster existence. Because when you win, you're a great coach in the eyes of the other people. And when you lose, you're a bum. It's a pretty hard way to live. And I think that if you're anchored in Christianity, there's a certain stability to your life that is not dependent entirely on external circumstances.

"I think Christianity provides you with a mission, with a purpose in your life that you will not find in any other way—whether it be in your profession, money, your family, or whatever. I think a sense of purpose has certainly been a very consistent theme. And then, I also think that Christianity gives you a certain sustaining strength and ability to do what you're required to do over a long period of time. Christianity is like an endurance race. It does give you strength. Your faith gives you endurance to see things through.

"I think that we are called to serve. The goal that has worked best for me is to honor God with what I have been given. I'm not saying that I have always been successful in doing so, but I have consistently tried in the way that I recruit, the way that I coach, that I conduct myself on the sideline to honor Him. That has give me a purpose and a mission and direction.

"Certainly, as you look around at the world today, you realize that we are existing in a tremendous mission field. And you don't have to go very far to find one."

And for Osborne, that mission field has been to build character into the lives of young men. That spirit within a student-athlete can be carefully fashioned as a diamond or harshly shattered as a clay pot.

"Probably the most important thing that happens in any football team or in any athletic program would be character development. I think the coach sets a certain tone and creates an environment. And if you hopefully create the right environment, you're more apt to see positive character development than in other environments. I think sometimes people in athletics can be damaged character-wise by athletic competition. I think that some environments are destructive and negative and tend to be counter-productive in that manner.

"I have never taught a team to hate an opponent or a situation because hate and fear are so closely related. And one can turn into the other so quickly. A team that loves each other will play very hard and very well. So hopefully we've set the right environment, here."

Though he has encouraged players to develop their spiritual side of life, he has not attempted to evangelize them.

"We certainly cannot preach at or to players. We do provide a chapel service that's optional before every game. I think it's important that they be given the opportunity to understand what Christianity is all about and make a decision for themselves."

The native of Hastings, Neb. traced the roots of his spiritual journey to the summer of 1957. Osborne had been raised in a Christian home and was the grandson of a Presbyterian minister. His personal faith in God was something he valued, yet it bore minimal vitality in his everyday life. But between his sophomore and junior year at his hometown college, his perspective changed when he attended a national Fellowship of Christian Athletes conference in Estes Park, Colorado.

"During that week I heard Christianity articulated in a way I could relate to better than I ever had before. I reached a stage in my personal life where I was very receptive to that message.

"I can't put an exact date or time on it, but I'm sure it was during that conference that I would trace my mature commitment as a Christian to. I just made a commitment at that time and I've really never wavered from that commitment since.

"I really wasn't turned off [to Christianity prior to that camp]. Though I had grown up in the church, I was not a committed believer. I think the faith I had was more that of my parents than my own faith. I think at some point each person has to decide for themselves what it is they believe rather than what their family believes. At that time I really thought things through for myself and Christianity became my own faith."

The head coach since 1973 and a staff member of the Cornhusker football program since 1962, Osborne has borne a rich athletic career.

A multi-sport prep athlete at Hastings, Osborne was named the Nebraska High School Athlete of the Year in the mid 1950s. Recruited by Nebraska, the quarterback opted to play both football and basketball at his hometown college. He was named the State College Athlete of the Year in 1959.

The state's first athlete to earn both top prep and collegiate honors played three seasons in the National Football League. A wide receiver, Osborne spent his first two with the San Francisco 49ers and third with the Washington Redskins. He roomed with eventual Congressman and 1996 Republican vice-presidential candidate Jack Kemp during his time as a 49er.

In 1962 Osborne joined new head coach Bob Devaney's staff as a graduate assistant. He earned his doctorate in educational psychology in 1965 and was then hired as receivers coach in 1967.

A full-time assistant, Osborne schemed Nebraska's winning offenses leading up to the 1970-71 consecutive national championship seasons. He also helped mold 1972 Heisman Trophy wingback Johnny Rodgers on the field.

At age 34, Osborne was chosen by the retiring Devaney to succeed him as head coach in 1973. The legendary Devaney stepped down to serve as athletic director.

Though success has trademarked Tom Osborne's tenure with his teams annually finishing in the top-25 with at least nine victories during his 240-win plus career, he has endured varying criticisms for over 20 years. During the 1970s his teams [all finishing in the top 10], won a minimum nine games and played in a bowl annually, yet he was continually second guessed for not beating coach Barry Switzer's Oklahoma Sooners. During the early 1980s, three teams [1981-83] came within a whisker of the national championship. From January 1988 through January 1994, Nebraska teams lost seven straight bowl games. Three of those seven opponents won the national championship as a result. The nation briefly wooed Osborne following a 24-17 Jan. 1, 1995 national championship victory over the Miami Hurricanes. But that same year, en route to the team's second straight title, some members of the national media questioned Osborne's integrity by asserting that he was a "win-at-all-cost" coach.

But when people reflect on the highlights of Tom Osborne's coaching career, they think in terms of big games and national championships. Though he remembered those events, the Nebraska native placed more value on the process behind those games and seasons. Fans remembered the numbers. But he remembered the players and coaches and their commitment.

"It's never been quite so important to me to win a national championship as it has been to have a team play at that level. It was certainly a great event to win the national championship. Once you win it, there are banquets and celebrations and all those kinds of things, but it was actually the pursuit that seemed to be more meaningful to me," he said prior to the 1994 season.

Though Nebraska won back-to-back consensus national championships in 1994-95, a handful of other Osborne-coached teams have come close to winning titles as well.

"I have received a certain amount of satisfaction knowing that on at least two or three occasions I think we had as good of a team if not the best team in the country, or at least we played at that level.

"Sometimes you just don't win the trophy, but your performance is what counts and tenacity and maximizing your abilities and those kinds of things are really more critical, probably."

In the Jan. 2, 1984 National Championship Orange Bowl, Nebraska fell to Miami 31-30, coming within a failed two-point conversion attempt of winning. A decade later, another undefeated team lost to Florida State 18-16 on a last second field goal that sailed wide left.

Osborne said he felt no sense of deja vu between those two games.

"It was a different circumstance, a different game, so I didn't feel any sense of history repeating itself."

In 1984, Nebraska scored two touchdowns in the closing seven minutes to get within one point of the fourth-ranked Miami Hurricanes. Forty-eight seconds remained. Three-time All-Big Eight and Second Team All-America quarterback Turner Gill rolled right and fired a two-point conversion pass to running back Jeff Smith. Hurricane strong safety Ken Calhoun deflected the missile as it bounced off Smith's pads incomplete.

Ten years later, Osborne's Cornhuskers found themselves in the same stadium and facing the same end zone where the conversion pass had been denied. It was Jan. 1, 1994 and No. 2 Nebraska trailed top-ranked Florida State by a deuce following a Seminole field goal with 21 seconds remaining. On the ensuing drive, Husker sophomore quarterback Tommie Frazier completed a 29-yard pass to tight end Trumane Bell inside the Florida State 30. Officials initially allowed the clock to expire after Bell was tackled. But after conferring, referees tacked one second on the board, allowing for a 45-yard field goal attempt.

Drenched in his team's Gatorade following a premature victory celebration, Seminole veteran coach Bobby Bowden nervously awaited the final play. Husker kicker Byron Bennett's attempt sailed wide as Nebraska left the field saddened, but proud.

"I felt that things were very chaotic and I was just trying to make sure everybody kept their heads and that we had an opportunity to at least kick the field goal. Unfortunately, we didn't make it. But, I was proud of the way the team played and they kept their heads up after the game was over."

Following that loss, Osborne was still criticized for never having won the elusive title. But it did not shake his contented demeanor.

"If the field goal goes through, we make three more points and we win the National Championship. I don't know that that would have made a whole lot of difference to me. I think, as a coach, I had done everything I could. I think the players had done everything they could. The ball just didn't happen to go through the uprights. I guess I would be pleased, naturally, but the main thing to me is that we played well enough to win the Championship. We were at the top level of college football. And there has to be a certain amount of dedication and commitment to excellence to do that. Winning or losing isn't as critical as playing well."

And his words prior to the 1994 season were prophetic.

"The difference between that Orange Bowl and what might happen in the future probably would not be that much different to me."

As players, fans, and media applauded him following a Jan. 1, 1995 24-17 national championship win over Miami, Osborne's calm, business-like disposition did not waver. But laurels from the national media faded quickly for Osborne that same year.

According to Lancaster County Court documents, leading Heisman Trophy candidate running back Lawrence Phillips was charged with assault, trespass, and destruction of property relating to an incident involving his former girlfriend on September 10, 1995. The destruction to property charge was later dropped by the State. However, Phillips was convicted of the other charges after a plea of no contest. Nebraska players then reportedly unified with a determination that all team members would stay out of trouble from thereon.

Phillips, initially suspended from the team indefinitely, was reinstated six games later after Osborne decided that he responded well to counseling. Osborne said he felt the structure and stability of football was important in Phillips' life toward a hopeful recovery from his behavioral problem. According to Lancaster County Court documents, on December 5, 1995, Phillips was sentenced to one year probation. Public controversy grew as the preseason All-America candidate was selected to start in the national championship Fiesta Bowl, nearly four months following his initial suspension.

"Some people believe that the way the Lawrence Phillips thing was handled was absolutely wrong. It sent the wrong message. It was not proper. And a lot of people who know I'm a Christian were probably turned off. But through that situation, some people began to see that God is a God of a second chance. That every person is acceptable in His sight. No one can do anything so bad that we are cut off

from His love and acceptance. And that maybe there was a redeeming sense in that whole thing. I'm not asking people to say what I did was right or wrong. I don't know for sure what was right or wrong."

As he admittedly struggled to search for the best means of handling the situation. Osborne said he spent a lot of time in prayer and reading the Bible.

"From that point on I tended to walk each day a little bit more simply in the knowledge that God was going to have to take charge of things, And that He would. And that we could honor Him in every situation.

"It's very important to me to start the day with about 30 minutes of prayer. I try to pray again in the middle of the day. I also try to read the Bible during those times. This has been critical in my life.

"So when the things of the 1995 season began to crumble a

little bit, it's not like you're not prepared to some degree. And that's very important."

During the spring following that championship season, Osborne dealt with a blow of another magnitude–the accidental death of a player. On April 18, 1996, former quarterback Brook Berringer was killed in a tragic plane crash in a field near Raymond, Neb.

A somber mood overshadowed the Fellowship of Christian Athletes annual spring gathering that same evening. Berringer, along with other players, had been slated to speak to an estimated crowd of over 850 people. Coach Osborne addressed those in attendance that he desired to honor God amidst that tragic loss of a friend and former player.

"Sometimes it isn't pretty. Sometimes it's downright ugly. Sometimes it's horrible, like the events of today. But God can use every situation. And the question we have to ask is, 'How are we going to relate to that situation? Are we going to yield it up to Him and honor Him in the way that we meet that situation?'

"There is no question that we need to honor God, because that's what Brook would have wanted us to do. Absolutely no question. Brook honored God with his life."

And in like fashion, that steady purpose to honor God has stood as Osborne's guiding principle in life. The means to accomplish that end, of honoring God amidst all of life's circumstances, has been summarized in a scripture verse Osborne once read to his players. Prior to the 62-24 Jan. 2, 1996 National Championship Fiesta Bowl victory, Coach Osborne quoted 2 Timothy 1:7 to his team.

"For God did not give us a spirit of timidity, but a spirit of power, of love and of self-discipline." (NIV)

And it is in God's love, power, and self-discipline that Tom Osborne has striven to honor the Creator and persevere amidst the trials and glories of life.

Ron Brown
Man of Compassion and Convictions

Receivers Coach
1987-present

While the team reveled in their come from behind National Championship victory over Miami on Jan. 1, 1995, he sought out and consoled dejected Hurricane players.

Ron Brown is a man of bold compassion. The outspoken Nebraska receivers coach has carried his heart in his hands that he may share it with others.

"After the game, it was like a battle had just ended and the smoke had cleared. The Nebraska guys were rejoicing and celebrating. The Miami guys were beaten, wearied, and some with tears in their eyes. I felt a prompting from God to share my faith–to nurture them and meet them where they were at.

"I told one of the players, 'No matter how you feel, I know the Lord Jesus has a plan for your life.'

"It was a great place to witness. It just shows how God wants us to use every opportunity to share the love of our Lord and Savior so that others will want to live for and serve him."

Just six years prior, Brown found himself amidst a somber mission field. In January 1989 he prayed with and comforted a young recruit who was bedridden and dying of cancer.

Victor Stachmus, a touted offensive lineman of McAlester, Oklahoma was the first prep athlete of his native state to commit to the Cornhuskers. The 6-foot-5, 250-pound 18-year-old would never run into Memorial stadium on a game day, however. Two months after his February 1988 signing, he was diagnosed with lymphoblastic leukemia. He underwent chemotherapy and was confirmed to be in complete remission, but the malignancy returned to his body in July. He was sent to the UCLA Medical Center for further treatment.

"Victor Stachmus got very, very sick. The cancer began to spread through the rest of his body and began to invade his liver in a very serious way.

"Many people wondered, 'Would Victor Stachmus ever play football for the Cornhuskers?' However, I began to think, because of my relationship with Jesus Christ, and what I had done with Christ 10 years prior, 'Would Victor Stachmus enter heaven if God decided to allow his life to end?'"

Brown, who had personally recruited Victor, continued to visit him following the initial diagnosis. He felt compelled to share his faith with the dying young man.

Upon arriving at the hospital, the Stachmus family greeted him warmly. Brown asked permission to be alone with the teenager.

"What I saw was a very different young man. A young man who had been big, strong, and strapping with muscles and curly hair—just a wonderful looking person. All of that had disappeared. He was bald, his skin had turned green, his body was very sickly, and his weight had dwindled to about 190 pounds after being 250. My heart was broken. I fished for words. I didn't know quite what to say."

Admitting his helplessness aloud, Brown offered to share the message of the gospel—that Jesus Christ could give Victor Stachmus a peace of mind and victory over death. The youth wanted to hear it.

Brown opened his Bible and read aloud Romans 10:9-13.

"That if you confess with your mouth, 'Jesus is Lord,' and believe in your heart that God raised him from the dead, you will be saved. For it is with the heart that you believe and are justified, and it is with the mouth that you confess and are saved. As the scripture says, 'Everyone who trusts in him will never be put to shame.' For there is no difference between Jew and Gentile–the same Lord is Lord of all and richly blesses all who call on him, for everyone who calls on the name of the Lord will be saved." (NIV)

The pair then prayed together and Victor trusted Jesus Christ as Savior and Lord. Ron grasped the teen's weak hand. In the youth's debilitated state, moments of silence followed when Brown wondered if Victor was fading in and out of consciousness.

"When people are very sick," Ron recounted, "you're not quite sure they understand what they're saying. But when I opened my eyes, I saw tears streaming down his eyes. I knew that God had touched him in a very special way and he knew what he was doing."

Before returning home, Coach Brown purchased a Bible for Victor to read.

"I received a call from his mother about a week later saying that Victor had just died. But Victor had died with a Bible in his hand, she said, and the knowledge that he was going to heaven because he had received Jesus as Lord and Savior."

The conscientious receivers coach has regularly ministered to the less fortunate. Brown has founded six statewide Christian "I CAN" camps for disadvantaged children to attend each summer. He has also served as a Fellowship of Christian Athletes national spokesman for race reconciliation.

"There's a variety of races across the state, even in small rural towns," Brown said on the note of racial reconciliation. "There are increasing racial tensions beginning to permeate many communities. What better opportunities for Christians who have supposedly given this sin over to Christ? What better opportunity for them to provide the healing touch in these communities through Jesus Christ? The objective isn't to heal the races, but to heal the human heart through the love of Jesus. Races getting along should be a by-product of right Christian living."

The host of a weekly five-minute Christian radio program heard across the state, Brown has also been a strong advocate of the pro-life movement. His desires to help the unborn are rooted in his upbringing.

Brown was adopted as an infant from an orphanage in New York City by a nurturing couple in their forties from Vineyard, Mass. He knew he was blessed with life and opportunity.

His desire for race reconciliation arose from the example of a middle-aged benefactor he remembers as the late Mrs. Chinland.

"She was a wealthy white board member of an inner-city orphanage consisting primarily of black and hispanic children. And I was one of those children. And she saw to it that I was adopted by a loving couple. She went above and beyond the call of duty."

Even long after he left the orphanage as an infant, Mrs. Chinland sent him a birthday card with money in it each year. She later funded a a portion of his graduate school tuition. He says her example has burned in his heart when surrounded by circumstances that might have motivated him to be racially divisive.

Brown recalled a high school football coach who attempted to incite racial hatred to inspire player performance.

"He once suggested that we remember history and slavery and the oppression of blacks across the world. In this instance he tried to teach us how to hate, to play better. But it became very difficult to hate as I continually thought about Mrs. Chinland."

With those convictions taking shape, Brown graduated from Martha's Vineyard High School in 1975. And though he was raised in a religious environment by his adoptive parents, he openly rejected God until the closing weeks of his senior year at Brown University.

"Because of the sheltering that I had from my disciplined home, I decided to break loose and stop going to church and live my own life."

But, even away from church on the secular campus, well-meaning Christians endeavored to reach him with the gospel. Figuring they were simply weird religious fanatics, he openly rejected them. However, their words convicted him and he attempted to justify his attitude.

"I remember as a sophomore telling my roommate, 'I'm not even sure God exists.'

"I was really trying hard to figure out a way that God would not exist. I was looking for reasons not to come to Christ. Yet in my heart, I was as guilty as I don't know what.

"I had so many people hitting me with that in college for four years. I was kind of like a target, 'Man, let's go get Ron!'

"I think people saw something in me. They sensed that, 'This guy is kind of searching for something. He is basically a nice kid. He's a mischevious guy. He thinks he's a cool guy. But he's one of those guys that won't go over the edge. There's something restraining this guy. There is something inside of him that says he might be open to the gospel.'"

During his junior football season, Brown's abrasive attitude toward Christianity slowly shifted as he grew acquainted with a little known sophomore scout team player named Harry Walls. The lean underclassman shared a locker adjacent to Ron's.

The soft spoken wide receiver frequently provided sincere encouragement and compliments for Ron after a bad game or a grueling practice. But the proud all-conference defensive back wasn't accustomed to behavior like this. Initially, he felt the pleasant freckle-faced young man was somewhat strange. Brown even taunted him one Sunday noon when he quietly appeared in the school cafeteria dressed in a suit and carrying a Bible. Walls offered no comment and discretely walked on past. The upperclassman grew to privately respect Harry for his genuine zeal and quiet confidence. This man bore an inner peace and definite sense of purpose that Ron admittedly lacked. On the field he displayed a notable intensity level, in spite of his minimal athletic ability.

"No matter how hard he got hit, he would get up smiling," Brown recounted. "He was a tough competitor. You never heard him complain or swear.

"He never shared his faith with me, but he lived it so loudly that when others spoke about Jesus, I thought about Harry Walls."

The volume peaked over a year later when Brown realized he could not control his destiny in life. Walls had since transferred to seminary and Ron now missed his encouraging presence. It was April 1979 and the Ivy League's top defensive back felt his dreams of playing in the National Football League were fading before him. Coaches and scouts said Brown was a possible third round draft prospect. To his dismay, however, he was not chosen in any of the 12 rounds.

"I was devastated. I had an Ivy League diploma and a lot of

things going for me, but my thing was the applause of the world. It was a very ego-dethroning experience."

The insecure young man found himself sitting across the table from a scout for the Dallas Cowboys in a downtown Marriott Hotel restaurant. The businessman pressed him to sign as a free agent. Brown would not automatically make the team, but he could have the opportunity to try out.

"I felt really nervous and hurt at the time. I just wanted to be away from everybody. I had a spiritual problem. I had a career problem. There were just a lot of things that were up in the air in my life. Nothing was tied down, including me to that chair. So I got up out of that chair and walked away from that guy and asked for some breathing room.

"I got out in the hallway and said [to myself] 'Now is the time. This is the time that I need to rely on Jesus Christ and trust Him totally with my life.'

"I wasn't sure I said the exact proper prayer, but after I had prayed, I felt assured that God was with me and that I would some-day go to to heaven.

"I said, 'Wherever He leads me, I'm going.'–Nothing else was tied down, but now my relationship with Jesus was."

With a renewed vigor, Brown signed with the Cowboys as a free agent. But to his dismay, he was cut a week later after failing the physical due to a bad shoulder.

In July he was invited to the New England Patriots training camp. Brown was eager to play for his home state team. But the rookie lacked the necessary focus to compete.

"I was playing bad because I was comparing myself with every-one else. Before I knew it, I wanted to leave camp. I was so miser-able and so worried about what other people were thinking. I even asked the coach to put me on waivers and to cut me and send me home. And he did so."

That fall, the frustrated athlete determined to put his gridiron aspirations behind. He enrolled at the Columbia University School of Public Health to earn a masters degree in health and hospital administration.

"However, the Lord had football planned for me all along and he kept it in my heart," Brown recalled.

The graduate student joined the semi-pro New Jersey Rams for the 1979 campaign. The following season he signed with the New York Jets. A week later he was cut again. A muscle pull sidelined him this time. His self-esteem languished as he received the nick name "Slice" because of his ill-fated attempts at a professional career.

"I had to go back home and face family and friends and people looking at me funny and thinking that I was a failure. I had to search deep inside and decide, 'What did God really have for my life?'

"But again, He brought the desire to stay with football. I began to train again and obey Him in this area."

In 1982 he completed his masters degree. His parents could not afford to attend his graduation, but an elderly Mrs. Chinland was there. An inspiration throughout his life, Brown recalls with pride how she participated in the ceremony with him.

"You should have seen the open-mouth stares from deans, faculty, and students as I, this 6-foot, 25-year-old black man, went down the aisle–arm in arm, one slow step after another–with this 80-year-old, white-haired, icy-blue eyed white woman, half my size, to receive my masters degree."

With degree in hand, the NFL again beckoned that May.

"The Chicago Bears decided to take a chance on me. I was no longer a rookie in my performance. I knew what was happening in the world of pro football. I was performing well until one day in a drill when I twisted my knee as I landed on it awkwardly. There was no doubt in my mind that I had seriously hurt it!

"The Bears sent me home with an injured knee and I decided to pray to the Lord as to what He would have me to do with the world of football."

Chicago head coach Mike Ditka instructed Ron that if he could successfully rehabilitate the knee, he would receive another opportunity to play.

"Again, the desire to stay with football continued in my heart. Against all the odds and the funny looks from people, I continued to work out."

But the knee did not recover. Brown returned to the semi-pro team in New Jersey that same year, this time as a coach. He served as the Rams defensive coordinator and defensive backfield coach.

That spring, passion to play still burning, Ron attempted to play again. His venture took him to the Philadelphia Stars of the United States Football League. But the lagging knee injury traveled with him. Thus, his life in pro football terminated before he could play a down.

"And finally, my pro football career ended without me ever getting started.

"I couldn't understand what the Lord was doing. I felt like I was in a wilderness period. It certainly was a needed period. I drew close to the Lord during those times, but I received a lot of ridicule from so many people. I couldn't quite understand what God had for me in the game of football."

But his forte would not be as a player, but as a leader. He truly felt a calling to the coaching profession.

"God began to lead me into the world of coaching. That's what He wanted all along, little did I realize. He had to humble me and break me down to a degree and help me to understand that coaching was where he wanted me. Through a variety of circumstances under the sovereign greatness of the Lord God, He led me into coaching at Brown University and finally here to the University of Nebraska."

Brown embarked in his newfound career as the head freshman coach at his alma mater in 1983. He served as a varsity assistant the following two seasons and joined Tom Osborne's staff at Nebraska in 1987 as the receivers coach. He described the move to Lincoln as a divine opportunity.

"It was very ironic. I had never had any prior association with the state of Nebraska in any way. And most people that coach here either played here or coached high school ball in the state. So I knew it was a gift from God. I wasn't a household name. I was an Ivy League player that nobody knew about. But God inspired coach Osborne to open up an opportunity for me here.

"I'm not here merely to coach football, but I'm here to serve the Lord Jesus Christ from the platform of coaching football. Which means I use every gift and opportunity he has given me to boldly present and glorify Him in every aspect."

Since joining the Husker staff, Brown has turned down various coaching opportunities. Some of those jobs included a head coaching job at Brown University, coaching receivers at Florida State University and the Tampa Bay Buccaneers in the NFL.

In 1994 he graciously declined the offer from Bobby Bowden's National Champion Florida State Seminoles. Before a press conference, Brown summarized his reasons for staying in Lincoln.

"I'm simply a person that wants to do God's will. I love working for coach Osborne. He's a great role model. He's taught me a lot. I love my players. I love teaching Nebraska receivers and working with them in regard to being all-around players.

"In the Bible [it says], 'Don't work for the food that perishes, but rather the food that endures and has lasting value forever.' (John 6:27)

"For me, what has lasting value is my investment in my work and ministry in the state of Nebraska. I feel like I have poured out my heart to the state. I feel very involved. Coaching has given me a platform to do that.

"I don't want to live my life for the next promotion. I came here because I really felt this was God's place for me. This was where He wanted me. So, He can take me anywhere He wants me to go. I'm going to put Him first and let the chips fly and weigh each decision as they come along."

And since that pivotal decision to accept Christ at age 22, Brown has continued to let the chips fly as he endeavors to minister in each mission field he is placed.

"We are called to live out the gospel radically. And to do that in today's culture means getting out of your comfort zone!"

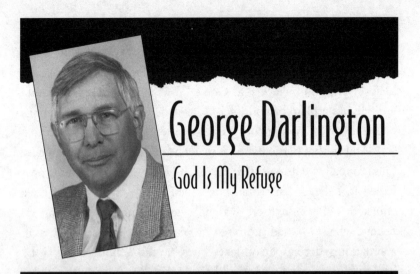

George Darlington

God Is My Refuge

*Defensive ends coach 1973-85,
defensive backfield coach 1986-present*

He was without a job, yet he dwelled in God's peace. The 1972 season had come to a close as George Darlington and the entire San Jose State football coaching staff had just been fired.

"I had three children, and no job. We got one month's salary. That was a time when it should have been extremely stressful. But my wife and I both had tremendous peace, concerning God's leading. And one of the verses, which to me is extremely meaningful, is, [Romans 8:28] 'All things work together for good to those who love God, who are called according to His purpose.'

"It wasn't just words. It really had tremendous meaning, because God's promises are true."

Raised in a southern Presbyterian home in West Virginia, Darlington accepted Christ as a teenager. But until that firing, his faith lay dormant.

"I think, the thing about the firing really brought to life, 'OK now, do you truly believe what you say you believe?' It's one thing when there's never any confrontation, when there's never any testing by fire, so to speak. You can espouse anything you want. You can say, 'I believe this, or I believe that.' But it was one of the times that really brought home, 'Do you really believe what you say you believe? Do you believe that God's Word is true and it's accurate and He has a plan for your life? Or are you just saying these things because you heard somebody else say them.'

"And so that particular time really brought me to a point where I had to really be honest with myself. If I did not believe what I professed to believe that would have been a time that I would have chucked it. Because there was no reason, humanly speaking, to believe what God had promised in His Word. Because if you're in a situation where a person loses his job, who is not a believer, he has nothing to cling to, I don't believe. You can take all the philosophical things, and there's no meaning to me apart from the Word and what God says. I mean, that's why we have people who are nonbelievers who have to find gratification in so many other areas because they have nothing of eternal significance to hang on to."

But Darlington's coaching career found promise when he joined rookie head coach Tom Osborne's crew at Lincoln as a full-time assistant in 1973. The former Rutgers two-platoon end and lacrosse All-American has remained a veteran staff member during Osborne's tenure. Darlington coached defensive ends his first 13 seasons and has directed the defensive backfield since 1986.

From unemployment on the west coast to a stable position in a top-25 program in the midwest, the move was somewhat miraculous in itself.

"There was no way, humanly speaking, that I should have ever come to Nebraska. Because Nebraska had come off of great seasons, they literally could have hired anybody that they had wanted within reason to be an assistant coach. And coaches out of work are not exactly hot commodities to go hire. And so, the fact that I am here is certainly due to the fact it was God's desire or will for my life, and my wife's life."

Though involved in a consistent program with a greater sense of job security, life's problems followed Darlington to the heartland as well. During the early '70s, George and wife Susan, again, together relied on their faith to weather an even larger storm. Their marriage vows, made in 1962, were on the verge of being broken in divorce.

"It really was a situation where both of us really had to depend on the Lord, and let God work it out, and for both of us to be submissive to allow the Lord to work His will out in our lives in this particular situation. There was nothing to cling to but God's Word.

"And then it was amazing to see how God brought two people, who were obviously at odds with each other, to a relationship and a marriage that was far better than they ever imagined it could be. That was obviously a profound time for both my wife and I."

In 1992, that same faith provided sustaining hope as Susan battled and beat cancer. The couple was again committed to trusting in God despite life's adversities.

"I had a great opportunity to witness to a lot of people because they couldn't understand why she had such a peace when, again, the big 'C' is the most frightening letter in our alphabet in American society. And that gave a negative an opportunity for a positive, because people were amazed at her confidence and her peace."

At the root of her confidence and peace was her faith in God, Darlington noted. It was a trust regarding that life is indeed hard, but God is good, regardless of circumstances.

"When people have problems, they, number one, are going to have problems. And number two, there's one source to handle the problems.

"[The apostle] Paul talked in Philippians [4:11-13] about how he was content in every situation. Whether he's high on the hog or in the mire, he's content in every situation. And the only way that we can come to that realization is when the Bible and God are alive in an individual's life."

Darlington said that God desires to build character into people's lives, thus the reason for trials.

"When you see God's truth, God's perspective on life, and God's promises—you understand that there will be trials and testings. It's not a shock when they happen. And you are naive to think that they are not going to happen. And then it's a matter of who do you depend on? What is your confidence based on? Is it based on money, position, personal power or is it a humbling situation that you base it strictly on the fact that God's Word is true and Jesus is the Rock? That's what you should base your confidence on. Because from a human standpoint, when certain things happen, there really is nothing, humanly speaking, to base it on. It isn't rational from the world's perspective."

Darlington also stressed the need for persistence in the Christian life and as a coach. The steady progress of the football program has been a symbol of perseverance for him. The assistant coach has witnessed and helped script Cornhusker drama spanning three decades under Osborne.

During the 1970s, with former head coach Bob Devaney a legend of past greatness, the program remained a consistent top-10 marvel. Yet, the Huskers frequently struggled to match up to

Oklahoma. Under the leadership of three-time All-Big Eight quarterback Turner Gill and company, during the early '80s, Nebraska narrowly missed winning a national title three times. And through following seasons, the Cornhuskers continued to reign within the top-25, but winced through seven straight bowl losses. Those defeats included a two-point Orange Bowl loss to '93 champion Florida State. But in 1994-95, the program built a two-year 25-0 record for back-to-back consensus titles.

"There were teams that we were playing during those times that we didn't measure up to. And, so the idea was to problem-solve how can we measure up within the context of the rules so that we can be competitive and maybe even be dominant."

During Osborne's head coaching career the balance of power in Nebraska-Oklahoma rivalry has swung like a pendulum. The 1970s saw a dominance by Barry Switzer coached teams. The series record split at 5-5 during the '80s. The scale favored Nebraska through the '90s to the end of the Big Eight conference.

"I think part of that has come from just persevering. And I think people would have to agree that we have persevered during that time and taken negatives and losses and allowed that to stimulate us to figure out a way to turn the bad situation into a good situation in the future."

Close controversial losses during national championship caliber games were frustrating, but also provided incentive to keep improving.

"Obviously, there were some bitter times in the '80s, where we lost a game or two where outside influences were involved. That was hard to accept. But by the same token, we were able to persevere and continue to improve our program."

Along with the title loss to Miami on Jan. 1984, six-of-seven straight bowl losses spanning the 1987-1993 seasons were to Florida teams. Those bitter New Year's Day losses, over half of them in the Orange Bowl, were again used to problem-solve and improve upon.

"We certainly learned a lot of what we feel is necessary today to be ultimately successful on the field by losses to the Florida teams. We obviously had to play them in tough places, but some years they were just flat out better than us. And many times, much faster than us. So, it accelerated our recruitment of people that can fly so that we can compete with them."

Though Nebraska lost to Florida State in the Jan. 1993-94 trips to Miami, they were no longer being dominated. The Cornhuskers were gaining an edge.

"We were in an extremely competitive situation, even though we lost."

With national championship wins over potent Miami and Florida teams, perseverance abounded generous fruit as Nebraska cruised to a 36-1 record over three years.

"The national titles were nice because we no longer had to be asked about not winning one. The perception of the sports world was that we could never win the big one, even though the facts didn't point that out. If you evaluate the teams we have beaten down through the years, you realize that we have won big games. The national championship was a goal that was accomplished, but then you set other goals. You set a goal to do it again."

Thus, good stewardship in every facet of life is essential, he said.

"I think it is wrong to not focus on doing the very best you can in whatever you do. It talks about in Colossians [3:23] and other places, about doing your work heartily as for the Lord rather than to men. It constantly talks about working to serve Christ. Even if your boss is not here, there's no excuse for deciding to take the day off. You should be focused and motivated to be a good witness even in the mundane things of life, such as working for a living."

Serving as an assistant at the same school since 1973 could be construed as mundane or being in a rut by some. But for Darlington, the biggest reason for staying has been contentment.

"I've had desires to be a head coach. And maybe I have not been as aggressive pursuing a head coaching job as maybe I should have if I wanted to be one. But by the same token, I felt that if God really wanted that to happen, the motivation would be there and the opportunity would be there.

"It's a hard program to leave. There aren't that many really good jobs, after having been at a place like Nebraska, that you would necessarily want. But it's like anything in our life, if the door is open and if God motivates you to go somewhere or if things happen where you are forced to go somewhere, you adjust and respond to it."

As Darlington has continued to seek God as his source of refuge and strength, he has hoped to be able respond to the daily challenges of life for his Savior's honor.

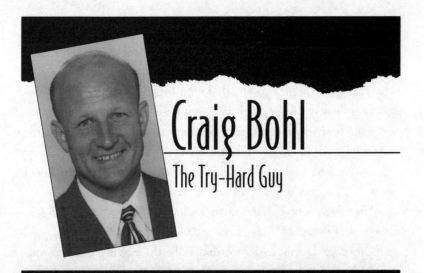

Craig Bohl

The Try-Hard Guy

Nebraska inside linebackers coach
1995-present, reserve Cornhusker defensive back 1977-79

Inside linebackers coach and Lincoln native Craig Bohl returned to his alma mater in 1995 after helping turn around floundering football programs at Rice and Duke.

A former Husker reserve defensive back during the latter 1970s and an experienced assistant coach, Bohl joined Fred Goldsmith's newly assembled Rice staff as the defensive coordinator in 1989. The rebuilding process there would be difficult, but fulfilling.

"When our staff first came in at Rice," Bohl remembered, "the program hadn't won a game in two years and the administration was contemplating dropping football. So it was a very risky situation. I was 28 years-old at the time and had never been a defensive coordinator.

"It's hard when these guys hadn't viewed themselves as winners, they didn't have a lot of athletic ability and really lacked confidence. We had a staff that really wasn't familiar with one-another.

"So we pressed very hard. And I think through those first couple years where we'd get beat 65-7, we knew that if we were teaching the right things and coaching the right way, that sooner or later things would turn around.

"And as a result of that, just spiritually and character-wise, I experienced a tremendous amount of growth.

"The world judges you by that won-loss record and a lot of university presidents only judge you that way, too. I don't think that that's the best way. I think, as a coaching staff, we were committed and convicted to doing the best that we could and striving for excellence. And we ended up having two winning seasons. And I guess that's something I'll always remember."

After five years with the Owls, including a latter pair of 6-5 seasons, Bohl followed Goldsmith's path to Duke in 1994.

The Blue Devils had recorded only three wins the previous year and were picked to finish last in the Atlantic Coast Conference. But under Goldsmith and company they tied for second and finished eight-and-four with a bowl game. The post-season contest was the school's first trip in five years.

"I worked with Fred Goldsmith, who's a really neat Christian coach. We went to Duke and tied for second in the ACC. It was a fun year. I really have fond memories. It was a lot of hard work."

Meanwhile in Lincoln, the Huskers wrapped up their first national championship season in 23 years and were gearing for a repeat. Only weeks following their Orange Bowl win over Miami, six-year inside linebackers coach Kevin Steele accepted a similar position with the Carolina Panthers in the NFL. Bohl, who had served as a UNL graduate assistant with linebackers and the secondary from 1981-83, inquired with Coach Osborne about the vacancy.

"I had heard that coach Kevin Steele, who I had known for a lot of years, had taken a job in the NFL. It was something that he was really excited about. And so I expressed my interest to coach Osborne. I wasn't completely set on moving from Duke, but I at least wanted to visit with him about the job.

"It really wasn't a situation where I needed to become familiar

with the surroundings or where the people really didn't need to become familiar with me. We had established a relationship over the last 15 years.

"But I think maybe it was just a confirming factor for me to come back and for the rest of the guys to see how we'd interact, and that went very well. As a result of that, coach Osborne offered me a job to coach the linebackers here. And I think it was a very good marriage.

"I know that losing Kevin Steele was a big loss. And I'm sure Kevin was an outstanding coach and a great recruiter who really worked out well with the staff and I knew had big, big shoes to fill and I probably haven't filled those shoes. But I think, as far as continuity purposes, coach Osborne felt it was the best way to go."

And assisting Osborne with one of collegiate football's greatest team's ever, during his first year back in Lincoln, was truly unique in itself.

"That was fun. I think back, I was a coach on a 1-and-10 Wisconsin team once. It was drastically different.

"I think 1995 was a very gratifying season. That night when we played Florida was a gratifying night. Because we had a football team that was talented, but they were very focused. I think our coaching staff devised a good game plan. But our players were really focused. They knew the plan and they put it to work out on the grass. They made it happen. And a lot of times, that does not happen. So that was rewarding.

"It was also rewarding to see how our players worked through all the adversity that year. They never turned on one another. It was really encouraging to be behind closed doors and see all the dynamics of what was going on. That was very rewarding—much more so than all the wins that we had. Yeah, we went 12-and-0 and no one even touched us, but it's those other things that I'll remember more."

Bohl has also appreciated the fellowship among Christian coaches.

"I think there's a strong Christian spirit within our coaching staff. Since I've been back, that's really been encouraging to be around other believers that have a chance to build you up.

"I think in any organization you're going to be characterized by the leader of the group. And I've really noticed that over the years since I've been here as a player and as a grad assistant, that coach Osborne has always had a strong faith. From that perspective it's really been a good move."

Looking back on his playing days from 1977-79, the reserve secondary player was philosophical.

"Football-wise, I really didn't have a great career here. I had a great experience.

"I was injured a couple times. I was a guy who didn't play very much but I was able to contribute to the team. I was a pretty marginal guy, athletically—a try-hard guy who knew what the game was all about. And maybe because of those limitations and being hurt, just really never experienced much playing time.

"However, I think because of that, I think God had a plan in that. I think He made me a little bit more empathetic to players that are injured. So, I think also in being involved in this program, it got my feet on solid ground as far as a coaching philosophy. And having a chance to play and then be a graduate assistant under Tom Osborne was a great experience. I think I was blessed by starting my coaching career out here."

A product of Lincoln East High School, Craig Bohl walked-on to the Big Red program as a reserve defensive back with a newly found Christian faith.

He accepted Christ the summer prior to his freshman season through the outreach of the Fellowship of Christian Athletes.

"Through that ministry I really came to recognize how deficient I was. I really knew there was no hope for me, but to put my trust in Jesus Christ. Which I did. And I experienced a tremendous amount of spiritual growth as a freshman and sophomore and through my years here."

Two upperclassmen, All-American defensive end George Andrews and quarterback Tom Sorley served as spiritual role models and mentors to him.

"Some older guys on the football team, like George Andrews and Tom Sorley, took some younger guys under their wing and we were involved in Bible studies and things like that.

"A lot of times I think you're just trying to grapple with who you are and where you're going. Football was so important to me. But I also saw how unstable all that was.

"I saw some guys who you would think had reached the pinnacle. And these guys would say, 'I'm all the way up at the top here and this isn't such a big deal.'

"So, I really saw a peace in a couple of the older guys who happened to be our team's captains: defensive end George Andrews and quarterback Tom Sorley. Their perspective on life was very attractive. They enjoyed life and they lived it to its fullest and had an abundant life.

"So, as far as their witness, maybe they had no idea, but I think they had a very powerful influence upon me.

"I noticed that my life began to change," Craig explained, "the language that I used; how I interacted with other people; some of the desires that I had in my heart.

"That did not mean that my old self didn't come back every once in awhile. But I did notice that I began to change from the inside-out.

"It was a neat time to see how God was working in my life and how He was changing me and how enjoyable that was."

As a sophomore, Bohl moved up the depth charts to second team. But his playing career would take a nose-dive following an injury suffered during a preseason practice. As a result, Bohl would spend eight months in a cast and considerable time in rehabilitation. He noted that, though the incident and recovery process were incredibly frustrating, positive fruit was yielded nevertheless.

It was August 1978, and the tenth-ranked Cornhuskers were preparing for their opener with Bear Bryant's No. 1 Crimson Tide at Alabama.

"We were working a cut-block drill and I got my lower leg shattered. I can remember the bottom of my foot dangling, saying "Adidas" [on the shoe]. I was scared. I was laying on the field and I didn't know what was going to happen. And in retrospect, all I really had was a broken leg. But to the person it happens to, you see your leg just flopping around. But I can remember being really frantic. And a coach on our staff, Rick Duval, who was a Christian came up to me and put his hand on mine. And he said, 'Craig, you know Who you need to go to.'

"And there was a real peace that came over me. Because I knew at that time, just through reading God's Word, that I was not going to be placed in any situation that God was not going to allow me to overcome. And He was going to give me the strength to deal with it."

Bohl said he later lay in a hospital bed feeling sorry for himself.

Duval entered the room with a word of encouragement. The assistant described how an intern team trainer became a Christian as a result of seeing the change in Bohl's spirits following the injury.

"Duval said that a guy saw what happened when he came up. And [the trainer] saw the peace that came over me. And he said [to Duval] 'I don't know what that guy has or what you did, but I want what that guy has. I've never seen that.'

"And Rick had a chance to witness with this guy. And the guy came to know Christ through that experience. And maybe it was that opportunity to open that door. I think that God works in all kinds of different ways. And that was reassuring to know that God was using me."

Proverbs 3:5-6 is a favorite portion of scripture for coach Bohl. It reads, "Trust in the Lord with all you heart and lean not on your own understanding. In all your ways acknowledge Him, and He will make your paths straight." (NIV)

"The reason that's a favorite for me is that trusting in God is a continual thing. There's an initial time that you do it [trust], but that's something that has to be done over and over again. It's easy for someone who doesn't depend on God or others to simply take charge of every situation. Then that [trusting in God] is a hard thing to do.

"'Not to lean on your own understanding.' If you think you've got this whole thing whipped—you're a pretty smart guy and you're a pretty doggone good coach—I'm going to trust in me. It's hard to trust in the Lord with all your heart. That's a difficult thing to do.

"But that verse is very reassuring because Proverbs are truths. Those things are proven. And you can see how much better your life will be, maybe not financially or through recognition, but just as far as peace, contentment and doing what God wants you to do. You will experience an abundant life if you do that. It's kind of an 'if then' thing. But that verse challenges me; it strives to keep me in check; and yet it also comforts me."

And that trust in God has proven crucial during disheartening times as a player, through challenges as a coach, and in each area he has willingly relied on his Savior's wisdom.

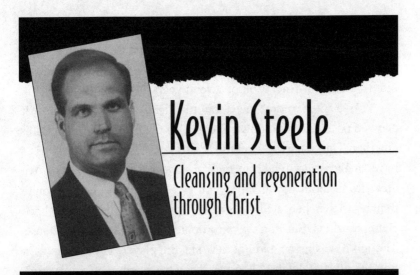

Kevin Steele

Cleansing and regeneration through Christ

**Inside linebackers coach
1989-94**

A business-like manner and friendly thick southern drawl distinguish the linebacker coach from Tennessee. Nebraska's inside linebackers coach from 1989-94 and currently an NFL assistant for the Carolina Panthers, Kevin Steele has loved implementing football defensive strategies as well as building into the lives of the game's players.

"God uses me to impact a particular player. Here in the NFL I can really share. There's a lot of fellowship here, and Christ is using me for His purposes.

"On the field, I think we need to be teachers. For defensive coaches, it's not like a chess game, it's like scrabble. You have to change on the run. The rules might be changed, so you have to adjust."

In 1993, Nebraska's defensive coaches changed a long-time philosophical approach in their front-seven player alignment. The retooling scheme would prove to be revolutionary en route to contending for the national title three straight seasons. After suffering through seven consecutive bowl losses, the staff recruited and implemented speed into the new attack-oriented defense. The switch to four down linemen and three linebackers revamped the old 5-2 read-and-react look of several years.

"We wanted more speed on the field," reflected Steele. "It allowed us to have two down linemen on the field and have a faster guy there, and have three off the line of scrimmage. It allowed us to have smaller guys, which in most instances, equates to speed. We grew from about as vanilla as you can get from it. I think, quite frankly, that it had a lot to do with producing the back-to-back championships. But don't give too much credit to the 4-3 defense. Though it was great, and got new life, the players could have won it in the 50 [5-2 defense] because those were pretty good players."

As the innovation of Nebraska's defense enabled the Blackshirts to dominate opponents in the mid '90s, Steele made a revolutionary move in his spiritual life some seven years earlier while a full-time assistant at Tennessee. In the early days of serving his alma mater, Steele recommitted himself to living for Jesus Christ. Though he became a Christian as a teen in the eighth grade, he said he never grew in his faith.

"The sad thing was there wasn't a prayerful study of the Word as much as there should have been. There was drift in and out; although my belief was there, my growth wasn't there.

"In 1986 I made the decision to change because enough was enough. This is not the way I was raised, this is not Christ's plan for me. I was raised in a Christian home with morals and convictions."

Leading up to that spiritual awakening, Steele admitted with regret that he "fell into the sinful ways of the world." The guilt from those actions left him empty and miserable. But upon confessing his sin to God and asking for His forgiveness, Steele said he found hope. Though his actions brought consequences, Steele said God graciously allowed him to leave his wrong doings behind so that he may strive to live above the power of sin.

"You have things that you have confessed, but you really haven't let go. And I realized that Christ died for my sins and that I don't have to keep having those things hanging on my back. I'm forgiven. And I don't have to let them drag me down. That was a big step in my Christian faith. That was a great burden lifted off. But there is still a big day-to-day challenge that you make decisions on a Christ-like walk.

"One of my favorite verses is John 19:30, when Jesus had received the sour wine [just before dying on the cross], and He said, 'It is finished.' If I could say anything to anyone that I think God would want me to say, it would be, 'It is finished' when you give your life to Christ. Start anew. Talk anew. And live anew. Because His last words on the cross were, 'It is finished.'"

The ensuing changes in his spiritual life were slow over time.

"It was a gradual process of change. And it still is. I'm not where Christ would have me yet. And I don't ever want it to stop being a gradual thing. Maybe that held me back in my Christian walk. I thought either you are there or you are not there.

"It's through prayer, every day and asking forgiveness and asking what's God's plan and what lessons has he got for me. It is truly a journey. It's not a destination. It's not saying you are going to be perfect. How you find strength and forgiveness is the key."

Steele said he also struggled with profanity on the football field. He knew it was tarnishing his example of how a Christian should conduct himself. He wanted to change for the better, and said he eventually did. But the Tennessee native said he found it hard to allow God to forgive him for those actions. It was especially difficult as others saw the contradictions in his life.

"In coaching you can develop bad habits such as spouting out profanity. That is something that has ceased. That used to tear at my heart and soul."

The coach said he found encouragement from the Old Testament in 1 Samuel 16:7 when Samuel was to anoint Israel's next king. Steele pointed out that he needed to see things from God's perspective.

The Lord said to Samuel, "Do not consider his appearance or his height, for I have rejected him. The Lord does not look at the things man looks at. Man looks at the outward appearance, but the Lord looks at the heart."

The football coach said he had confessed his wrong doings to God and had asked forgiveness. And it was now up to him to claim that forgiveness, Steele explained.

"Once we have given our life to Christ, the last part of that verse is the whole key, 'the Lord looks at the heart.' And once we have relinquished that and turned that over to God, it's done. God had forgiven me. And that has been one of the most peaceful things that I have gained as a Christian. I'm not going to let those things drag me back."

The Volunteer assistant served at his alma mater through the 1988 season and moved north to Lincoln in '89. At Nebraska he directed the inside linebackers through the '94 championship season. And while under head coach Tom Osborne, Steele said he learned what it meant to truly coach as a Christian should.

"Looking back, coach Osborne taught me how to be a Christian coach. It wasn't something he did intentionally. It's just God used him to show me that you can go out and teach without profanity and skirting issues and painting pretty pictures. He's not a preacher. He doesn't preach, he just lives it. He's an example.

"Coach Osborne's program is unparralled. Not many coaches have ever won as many games as Nebraska or been to as many bowls. When we finally won the national championship, it was great. But the greatest thing about it was the look in coach's eye. And I don't think it meant the world to him. Because the year before [following an 18-16 Jan. 1, 1994 National Championship Orange Bowl loss to Florida State] you saw the same look in his eye. How proud he was. We knew we had the greatest coach in America."

Steele summarized his respect for Osborne with these words shared at a speaking engagement.

"Many things are said and written about men from people who don't really know them. When I worked alongside Coach Osborne, I witnessed a man of integrity. A coach who is upright in his faith, sincere in his promise, faithful in his duty, loyal in his service, and honest in his speech. It is a blessing to have a Coach Osborne in one's life."

And thus the Carolina assistant has sought to pattern his approach to his work in a similar manner. And the move from Lincoln to Charlotte was not an easy one.

"I loved Nebraska so much. I had spent six years there. And it had kind of become home.

"It was a situation where I had a friend who became a head coach. We had been very close throughout the years. He had said that if he ever got a head coaching job in the NFL that he would like me to go with him. I had never really ever thought about it. And then he called. It's intriguing to be in the NFL and be near [9 miles from] home.

"Those things were factors [in moving] but we had grown to love Nebraska so much. So it was really hard.

"So I just turned it over to the Lord and prayed about it. And to be honest, I just felt like it was the thing to do. I can't specifically say that any one thing particularly drew me. Making the jump from college to the NFL was not it. Finances was not it. And when it came down to it, being closer to home was not even it. It just felt like when I went through prayer and petition, and turned it over to the Lord, 'This is what I have in store for you, go.' And so I did it."

And after leaving, Steele said he was not surprised Osborne filled his old job with former Duke defensive coordinator and linebackers coach, Craig Bohl.

"I know what kind of man he is. And it doesn't surprise me when the person doing the selection is Tom Osborne. Coach Osborne knows character and that's what he's looking for. And I think Craig was a fit for that."

But for the university coach of 15 seasons, Steele's move to the professional football ranks was not without its growing pains. He described how he went from being recognized state-wide in Big Red country to being little known, even in his own neighborhood.

"In college coaching you're put out front. You are always being interviewed. You're always in the news. And although the players and the head coach are very important, the assistant coaches get a feeling that it strokes your ego. And maybe too much so.

"In the NFL that is very different. It's obscurity at it's best. As an assistant football coach, except for the team members and a few avid fans, people don't even know who I am or care. It's different from having been an assistant coach at Nebraska. Everywhere you went, people knew that you were an assistant coach for the Nebraska football program. That's not the case in the NFL, anywhere. The assistant coach is just kind of an obscure figure that's in the background. And although that was very different, it has turned into something very positive. I think there's a Christian lesson in it. Maybe you had let your ego get too big and this is kind of a way of humbling that and putting that into place. What you do is not as important as your walk with Christ."

Steele added that the majority of a pro football assistant coach's time tends to be in solitude.

"Coaching in the NFL as an assistant is kind of a lonely job. You do a lot of work individually as far as game preparation. You're by yourself a lot. You're kind of stuck back in a corner and there's a little bit of a loneliness. Coming out of the program at Nebraska there was always something you were involved in. It was more of a team-staff concept. Where in the NFL you have specific things that you are individually in charge of. And you go do them and just get them done. There's a lot of paperwork, a lot of number crunching, and a lot of film watching and that is done by yourself. And the information is compiled later. Where at Nebraska, a lot of our work was done together."

But there have been definite dividends to be reaped within his current surroundings. A positive for the Tennessee alum has been the return to his native South to spend time with his family. Another plus within the Panther franchise has been a recent surplus of committed Christian players.

"Here there are many players who are very strong Christians and some are close to my age. And so I have all kinds of Biblical discussion with guys who have played in this league for a long time and have a wealth of Biblical knowledge.

"So it's fun to share with the players and grow that way. There's a lot more sharing and studying of the Word together from a player-coach stand point–and a lot of that is due to age. Because they are men, they aren't 18-to-22 year olds. And you don't have the barrier of the government with separation of church and state. It's not government-controlled where there are lines drawn that you don't do this or that. It is a private business."

And through his personal faith, he has been reminded that he can live in hope because of God's forgiveness. The forgiveness based upon Christ's finished work on the cross. And as his Lord stated, "It is finished," he too has desired to be a strong finisher in life.

"Life truly is a journey. It's not a destination. Life is filled with races. And all those things have an end result. There is a finish line. Life has a finish line, but we don't know where that is. So, as Christians we need to finish strong."

The Early 1970s
Setting the Standard

Back-to-back national titles in 1970-71, the 1971 Game of the Century–No. 1 Nebraska versus No. 2 Oklahoma in Norman. Indeed, the 1971 national championship team defined the criterion by which all future Nebraska teams would be measured.

Those two championship teams were comprised of eight All-American players, including offensive tackle Bob Newton, and I-back Jeff Kinney.

For those two athletes, that era of accolades was exciting, but not ultimately fulfilling. Kinney, who scored four touchdowns in the Game of the Century, related how God changed his heart from one of self-glorification to one that honors God.

"There was really no room for God in my life," Kinney said of his days as a Husker running back. "And I guess I would have thought that it [Christianity] was for people who were weak. If you couldn't do anything else, then you tried religion. It was kind of a crutch."

But his attitude turned in the spring of 1973, early in his NFL career with the Kansas City Chiefs.

"God really began to do a work in my life to give me a desire that I really wanted to be a better father and husband. 'But how am I going to do that?'"

"One of the scriptures that really convicted me and really stood out in my mind was 2 Corinthians 5:17. And it talks about becoming a new creature in Christ and the old things have passed away and behold all things have become new. And I really wanted to know in my life that I could start over, that my past could be forgotten about and that I could have a new beginning."

Bob Newton, who went on to a long NFL career, described how he overcame chemical dependency and has since become a counselor to aid those in similar need.

"I started my path back to the Lord. Getting the alcohol and the other drugs out of me and getting my head cleared up. I saw that I had to replace this lifestyle with the Lord. There was a void I had tried to fill up with booze, drugs, and football. I had to fill that up with my relationship with the Lord.

"I ended up eating with the pigs like the prodigal son before I finally came to my senses. The drinking and alcoholism is very powerful."

For both of these former All-Americans, discovering Christ's victory on the cross greatly surpassed their personal achievements on the football field.

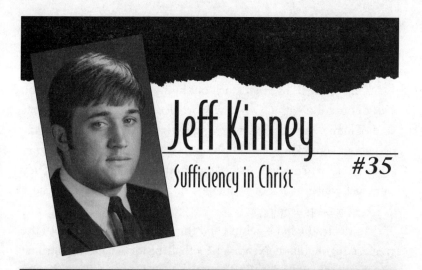

Jeff Kinney

Sufficiency in Christ

#35

With his shoulder pads flapping outside his tattered white tear-away jersey, the six-foot-two, 210-pound I-back from McCook pounded his way through No. 2 Oklahoma's defense. All-American Jeff Kinney finished that memorable afternoon with 171 yards and four touchdowns in the Game of the Century at Norman, Okla.

It was November 25, 1971, the day of what would be the most talked about game in Nebraska football history. Everything was at stake–the Big Eight and national titles. The Huskers, the defending national champions and ranked No. 1 since their second game of the season, faced their greatest rival.

"There was the buildup, No. 1 versus No. 2," recalled Kinney. "That began several weeks before it ever happened. We were always told to focus on each week's game and not worry what was coming down the road. That week of the game you could tell things were getting a little bit more tense. You could tell by the way the coaches were coaching, by the way they were hollering, and just the way that things were going."

In gearing up for the trip to Norman, the Nebraska football team took no chances in preparations on–and even off the field.

"One of the things that stuck out in my mind was that we took a lot of our food with us when we travelled to Oklahoma. That was kind of funny. I got a good laugh out of that. I think they were worried about some kind of food poisoning. It had happened before in a big game when some teams had gotten food poisoning. They were just concerned about gamblers or someone who might cause us to get food poisoning."

And with the hype behind and the game underway, one of the greatest highlights in Nebraska football history came in the first quarter. Johnny "the Jet" Rodgers, the 1972 Heisman Trophy winner, danced and skirted around defenders to return a punt return 72 yards for the opening touchdown. With 11:28 remaining in the first period, Nebraska led Oklahoma 7-0. Following an Oklahoma field goal two-thirds through the first quarter, Jeff Kinney scored the first of his hard-earned touchdowns. Just under four minutes into the second quarter, the I-back from McCook leaped over the pile at the goal line from 1-yard out.

But the Sooners rallied before halftime for the lead. Oklahoma quarterback Jack Mildren rushed for one touchdown and passed for a second prior to intermission. On his team's final scoring drive before half, he hit split end Jon Harrison with a 43-yard pass caught over the back. Next play, Mildren found Harrison in the end zone with a 24-yard pass completion to cap a 78-yard four-play drive with five seconds before the break. Oklahoma led 17-14 at the half.

Meanwhile, Jeff Kinney, who had been held to just 20 yards in the first half, found inspiration within the locker room. His team had been held to only 69 yards on the ground. That would change in the final 30 minutes of play.

"What really sticks in my mind is just the halftime, the determination that the guys took on in the locker room," Kinney explained. "Coach Devaney had a few inspiring words to say to us. Just the fact that we knew as seniors that we needed to win this game. The thought at the time was that our whole season didn't have much value if we didn't win this game. So I think everybody was just determined to go out and say, 'They're not going to stop us. We are not going to lose this game.'

"And we just carried that attitude out on the field in the second half."

The All-American exploded in the second half, carrying the ball 22 times for an additional 151 yards.

Nebraska retook the lead with 8:54 left in the third as Kinney crashed through the line, spinning and breaking a tackle from 3-yards out. All-American quarterback Jerry Tagge converted a key third-down-and-three with a 32-yard keeper on the play prior to Kinney's score. Nebraska led by four. The Cornhusker I-back added his third touchdown with 3:38 remaining in the same period from 1-yard out to extend his team's lead to eleven.

Not to be denied, Jack Mildren and the Sooners revived their magic. On Oklahoma's ensuing drive, Mildren faked a hand off to the running back and pitched back to his Harrison. The split end, with defenders in his face, fired a 51-yard pass to tight end Al Chandler to put the ball on Nebraska's 16. Four plays later, Mildren rushed into the end zone from 4-yards out. Twenty-eight seconds remained in the third quarter with the score, Nebraska 28, Oklahoma 24.

Approximately four minutes later, Oklahoma mounted their final scoring drive after recovering a Husker fumble at the Sooner 31. On the turnover, Tagge faked a hand off to wingback Johnny Rodgers but was wrapped up before he could pitch it to Kinney. With the ball bobbling between his back and left hand, the Husker signal caller lost it on the turf as he went down. And with 7:10 remaining in the game, Oklahoma took the game's third lead change on a 17-yard Mildren to Harrison pass to give the Sooners a 31-28 advantage.

Not to be denied, Nebraska returned with a smash-mouth 74-yard clock-eating drive that lasted nearly six minutes. Kinney carried the ball multiple times on that drive, highlighting it with a 17-yard run. The McCook native broke three tackles before being knocked of bounds around mid-field. The drive intensified as Nebraska pushed inside the Sooner 10. On second-and-six from the eight, Kinney carried defenders with him to the two. The ball squirted free as he hit the turf. But to the Sooner's dismay, the ball was ruled dead on the stop. One play later on third down, Kinney crashed through the end zone behind his fullback's block to give Nebraska the lead for good. With 1:38 remaining in the Game of the Century, Nebraska led 35-31.

Trailing by four, it was do or die for Oklahoma as they started from their own 19-yard line. But on third and six from their own 23, NU 1971 Outland Trophy winner and All-American defensive tackle Larry Jacobson broke through the line sacking Mildren back to the OU 15. Next play, fourth and long, the 1972 Lombardi Award and Outland Trophy winner middle guard Rich Glover hit Mildren just as he threw the ball, causing an incompletion. Nebraska took over on downs at the Sooner 15-yard line and ran out the clock. The final: Nebraska 35, Oklahoma 31.

"It was nip and tuck all day. We didn't know if we were going to win it or not. It was emotional after we won the game. The excitement was generated by the crowd coming out on the field."

One of Kinney's greatest memories of that afternoon was after the victory when he embraced his father at midfield.

"I ran into my dad who had gone down to the game. He gave me a big hug and took the rest of my torn jersey. It was neat for him to be there and for him to see it. It just meant a lot to me."

With the contest behind, Kinney could no longer block out the physical pain of the battle. He felt the effects of his hard-earned 171 yards on 31 carries en route to the airport.

"I developed severe cramps in my leg during the game in that last drive. On the bus, coming home [en route to the airport in Oklahoma], I was in constant pain. Both of my legs kept cramping and I couldn't get it to stop. But I didn't care much at that point because it was over with and we were on our way home."

Several thousand screaming fans converged on Lincoln's airport upon the return of their conquering heroes.

"I don't think we really realized the impact of that game until several years later. For me it was just a neat experience to see the people of Nebraska so excited, so involved in that event. I remember coming back from the Oklahoma game and 30,000 people came out to the airport. It was just a fun time."

The following week his team buried the University of Hawaii

in Honolulu. And on Jan. 1, 1972, top-ranked Nebraska flattened Paul "Bear" Bryant's then undefeated and No. 2 Crimson Tide 38-6 in the Orange Bowl. Kinney finished the national championship game with 99 yards and one touchdown. And with the win, the 1971 Nebraska squad came to be regarded by some analysts as the greatest college football team of all time.

Nebraska's 1970-71 championship teams were led by veteran coach, the late Bob Devaney. Kinney shared his feelings of the National College Football Hall of Fame coach.

"I thought Bob was a great coach. And I still think that. He just had a way to motivate people. He seemed to give his assistant coaches room to coach and he brought it all together.

"Everyone was so in awe of Bob, it just seemed that whatever he said had a lot of impact. He was very jovial and very friendly, but when you stepped on to the field, you knew that he expected certain things. He wanted people to have success."

As a Husker All-American, Kinney's personal pride was at a peak. The Cornhusker I-back who scored four touchdowns against Oklahoma in the 1971 Game of the Century had believed himself to be self-sufficient.

"There was really no room for God in my life. And I guess I would have thought that it [Christianity] was for people who were weak. If you couldn't do anything else, then you tried religion. It was kind of a crutch.

"Coach Osborne was a assistant coach then at Nebraska. I knew he was very influential [spiritually] to a lot of people, but I never paid much attention to it."

As a Cornhusker, the typically affable man of small town McCook, Neb. even shot down a teammate for discussing spiritual matters on the team bus.

"There were a couple guys who I had very little tolerance for, because they seemed to profess that publicly and lived it publicly. It just kind of antagonized me. I remember one time [running back] Joe Orduna was talking about religious things on a bus on the way to a game and I just told him, 'Why don't you just shut up and think about the game.'"

But near Christmas, during his first season in the NFL, the Kansas City Chief's first-round draft pick's attitude toward Christianity changed.

"Like a lot of people, I really felt there was something missing from my life. I thought that church might be the answer. So, like most people, I decided to go ahead and visit a church."

A pastor spoke with his family during a follow-up visit.

"Over the next three or four months God really began to do a work in my life to give me a desire that I really wanted to be a better father and husband just because of my lifestyle. I remember telling my wife 'I promise you I'll change. I'll be different.'

"During this time, I'm thinking, 'How am I going to do that?'"

His answer came when the church pastor visited a second time in March 1973.

"He led us through some scripture. One of the scriptures that really convicted me and really stood out in my mind was 2 Corinthians 5:17. And it talks about becoming a new creature in Christ and the old things have passed away and behold all things have become new. And I really wanted to know in my life that I could start over, that my past could be forgotten about and that I could have a new beginning.

"That night my wife and I both responded and said, 'We don't understand a lot of things about this, but we really know this is something we want in our life and have a need for.'

"By faith, my wife and I invited Christ to come into our lives. It was kind of a neat situation. It gave me a love for my wife that I never had before. It really was a dramatic change.

"That night was just really the beginning for us in our relationship, and in the relationship with our kids.

"I really believe God began to just open my eyes and give me the desires that I never had before. And as a result, he brought people into my life that shared the good news of how I could become a new creation.

"It gives you a sense of knowing that you need to be serving and ministering to each other as opposed to always worrying about your own needs. That was probably the biggest change right there. Having played football at Nebraska and then professionally, you kind of get the tendency to feel like your whole life responds around you and what you do. That caused a lot of pain. It was really just my own selfishness."

The following season, Kinney said he found spiritual strength through his friendship with split end Andy Hamilton.

"Andy and I both came in the draft in the same year. I was a first round draft choice and he was the second pick of the Kansas City Chiefs. I had played against him in the [Jan. 1971, National Championship] Orange Bowl. He was from LSU.

"It was late spring [1973] that I got a phone call from Andy. He said he heard the shock waves all the way down to Louisiana that I became a Christian. So we made arrangements that we would room together in that training camp. We spent some quality time together. He discipled me. He kind of watched over me on some things. We developed a good friendship that way."

On the gridiron, the Kansas City Chiefs had established themselves as an American Football League power in 1966 and as champions of Super Bowl IV in 1970. But in 1974 their rule crumbled amidst a 5-9 record. According to some analysts, several key players had likely spent their prime during the Chief's banner years. But Kinney explained that some team members and media felt the '74 squad's ailment was an alleged religious extremism.

It was during his third season with the Kansas City Chiefs, that Kinney said he and other teammates were accused by some of staging fanatical religious crusades within the club. Those alleged encounters supposedly caused team disharmony and ultimately led to the Chiefs first losing season in 11 years, he said. According to Kinney the charges were ludicrous.

"It was just crazy because there were a couple of players who said that it [Christianity] really bothered them," recalls Kinney, "but there were three of us. It was like they were trying to blame a lot of the problems Kansas City was having on Christianity. There were a couple of players that said it really bothered them to come down for a game meal and stuff like that and see guys in a Bible study and they said it just distracted them and broke their concentration.

"I'm not sure what they were thinking. I can't ascribe to what they were thinking or what they felt. But when people start losing, they always start pointing the finger."

Kinney recalled comments within an article in *Sports Illustrated* that, he said, pointed the finger.

"Some teams, notably the 1974 Kansas City Chiefs, have been disrupted by overzealous God Squaders trying to push hellfire and brimstone on the whole team." stated an April 19, 1976 article in *Sports Illustrated* entitled "Religion in Sport."

The Chiefs 1972 first round draft pick noted that he and his Christian teammates did not attempt to confront others about the Bible or preach at them.

"There were times when we would have a study in our room at night. The only people that wanted to come would come. It seemed like a couple of times guys were looking for the stag films and hit our room instead. They opened the wrong door.

"I just think there were a couple of guys that knew me and knew what I was like and they made several comments like, 'I had a neighbor who tried religion and it wore off in a couple years.'

"I think it was that kind of an attitude that they had seen this kind of stuff and it hadn't worked. There were several articles that were written in the papers and there were several interviews, but it wasn't like we were brow beating anybody or sharing with anybody."

Kinney recalled when a teammate confronted he and Andy Hamilton.

"I remember one time, Andy and I were sitting there, getting taped and he walks up to us and he said, 'I'd rather be a king in hell than a slave in heaven.'

"Andy and I just kind of looked at each other in disbelief. Once again, we hadn't really shared anything with him. It was just that he had known some things about us and you never know what's being said behind the scene."

Nevertheless, the difference in his and Hamilton's life style was evident.

Kinney remained with the Chiefs through 1975. After being cut, he played the following season with Buffalo and retired in '76.

As the former running back from McCook has reflected on his days since that famous afternoon in Norman in in 1971, Kinney can honestly say that far greater things have happened in his life.

"I'm thankful for the career I've had and where the Lord has brought me."

The former All-American currently resides in Chicago, Ill. and serves First Albany Corporation as the vice president and manager of their capital markets division.

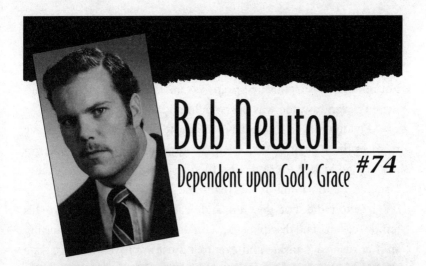

Bob Newton

Dependent upon God's Grace #74

Consensus All-American offensive tackle 1970,
All-Big Eight offensive tackle 1970, 1970
NU offensive captain, two-year letterman 1969-70

The former All-American offensive tackle found a new lease on life after nearly 20 years of addiction to drugs and alcohol. Bob "Big Fig" Newton was an imposing six-foot-four, 248-pound lineman from La Mirada, Cal. who anchored the 1970 Nebraska national championship team's front line. The west coast native and 10-year NFL veteran lived hard and fast. He started drinking at age 14 and began smoking marijuana during his senior year of high school. That lifestyle would change on July 12, 1983 upon entering a treatment center. The former pro lineman eventually returned to his alma mater and earned a bachelor's degree in community health. And upon seeing a chance to help those who similarly have fallen to substance abuse, he committed himself to service as a drug and alcohol dependency counselor and speaker. All along the way, his life would follow the path of the gridiron.

Newton's first steps on to the football field were at age 15 as a sophomore, upon the prompting of his school athletic director. The youth had been arrested twice and was failing two classes. He needed something positive to preoccupy his time. The drive and ability that would define his tenure as a seasoned professional was not remotely visible his first prep season. The chunky youth's skills weren't even raw. He was overweight and uncoordinated.

"I hadn't played football as a youngster. I was always too heavy to meet the weight class. I went out my sophomore year and got my behind kicked every day by the varsity. I could hardly get into a stance. I almost quit. It was really tough."

Newton did not give up and learned proper technique his junior season. The discipline paid off as he earned a varsity starting spot at defensive tackle and eventual most improved honors. As a senior, Newton garnered all-area and conference accolades. But with only a pair of colleges paying noticeable attention to his abilities, Newton enrolled in Cerritos Junior College.

After earning All-America status at Cerritos two years later, several major universities showed interest in his abilities, he said. Among the potential recruiters, then assistant coaches Barry Switzer of Oklahoma and Tom Osborne of Nebraska contacted him. He liked Osborne. To this day he can recall their first meeting when the Cornhusker assistant's tall thin silhouette appeared in his doorway. Upon visiting Lincoln, he discovered he did not enjoy minus 10 degree winter weather. The school of the midwestern plains was not for him, he thought as he returned home. Besides, the California kid's dream was to play for USC, which he said initially offered a scholarship.

Two weeks prior to signing date, he realized he had not heard from Southern Cal in some time. He contacted their coaching staff to verify where his future stood. But with one phone call, his longing loyalty to the Trojans turned to spite.

"I hadn't heard anything, so I called them up and I asked for the coach that I had talked to. He put me on hold and then came back with some excuse that I had something wrong with my transcripts.

But it was just a way to get out of it. Because there was nothing wrong with my transcripts. That really angered me.

"Nebraska had USC on their schedule two years in a row [1969-70]. So, I said that if I can't play with them I'm going to play against them. That was a huge part of the reason I went there. I had a huge resentment toward USC. And I wanted them to understand what they were passing up. And I also went because of my admiration for coach Devaney and coach Osborne."

At UNL, Newton earned his nickname, "Big Fig" from a teammate while hanging out in the campus dormitory. The label stuck permanently.

"'What's your name?'" the conversation went.

"'Bob Newton.'"

"'You mean, like Fig Newton.'"

"'No, it's Bob Newton.'"

"'Well, I like Fig Newton.'"

And the name stuck as the rest of the team adopted it for him, as did Nebraska's sports information department. Newton good-naturedly accepted the label. The title even appeared on his NFL football cards over the years. Pro teammates eventually called the veteran lineman "Papa Fig" as his career lengthened. Hoping to gain commercial endorsements from his nickname, Fig said he sent Nabisco Foods, Inc. pictures of himself in his Chicago Bears uniform with a note explaining there was a real Fig Newton in the NFL. Newton laughed in reflection that he never received a response.

As a new Husker lineman, the Big Fig played during the fourth quarter as a backup during his team's 31-21 loss to fifth-ranked USC on Sept. 20, 1969. Newton took over the starting reigns eight games into the season against Iowa State.

The Huskers finished 1969 at 9-2 and ranked eleventh by Associated Press. It was Nebraska's best record since 1966 after going 6-4 two straight seasons. Newton said many media representatives touted Nebraska as one of the top three teams in the country despite their final ranking.

Going into the next fall, Husker players grew hungry for something unprecedented at their school—a national championship.

"We went into training camp in 1970 to go for a national championship. We felt that strong about our team.

"We really had the concept of a team. Everyone cared about one another and would sacrifice for their teammates. Today I see a lot of individualism in team sports. I really felt that we represented the definition of 'team' that year."

Following a 36-12 whipping of Wake Forest in the 1970 season's home opener, the No. 9 Cornhuskers travelled to Los Angeles to face third-ranked USC. Sept. 19 had long been marked on Newton's calendar.

"USC had just obliterated Alabama the week before. They ended up tying us [21-21]. It was a great game. Our offensive line dominated them. We ran the ball up and down the field. Even though we didn't win the game, I had made my point. I looked over at their sidelines when we were dominating on the ground and running the ball down their throats. I looked at their head coach, and kind of gave him a twinkle out of my eye, like 'You could have had me!'" Fig laughed.

"They were mad that they didn't beat us. That was our only blemish that year and we went on to win the rest of our games."

Meanwhile, regardless of his on-field success, Newton's lifestyle brought him turmoil. Bob and his wife struggled through their new marriage as he continued to drink heavily. His wife contacted a local church pastor who, in turn, paid a visit.

"I came home from practice one day and he was there to offer counseling to us. He shared the gospel and we asked the Lord into our lives. I was sincere, but I didn't have a huge big bomb go off.

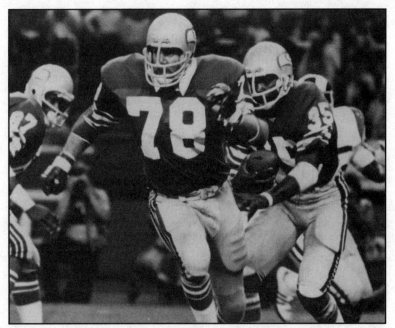

There wasn't any follow up. I didn't make a commitment to read the Bible or go to church. I continued to use alcohol. I continued to live a wild life."

On the gridiron, the offensive tackle earned first-team All-America and all conference honors. The 1970 Huskers finished the regular season undefeated and went into the Orange Bowl ranked third behind top-ranked Texas and No. 2 Ohio State. But with upsets to the Longhorns and Buckeyes on New Years Day, it set up an opportunity for then third-ranked Nebraska to play No. 5 Louisiana State for the national title. In the Cotton Bowl, Notre Dame upset Texas 24-11 as Stanford beat Ohio State 27-17.

"We watched the Cotton Bowl and Notre Dame upset Texas. Our game was the last game of the day. Now it was just Ohio State and Nebraska left who were undefeated. [1970 Heisman Trophy winning quarterback] Jim Plunkett and the Stanford Cardinals upset Ohio State. We found out the final score when we were on the bus to the Orange Bowl. And the bus just erupted with enthusiasm. Everything fell into place. And I say it was by God's grace."

Over 80,000 fans filled the Orange Bowl stands to watch that New Years night national championship game. The Huskers drew first blood late in the first quarter. With 2:40 left in the period, Nebraska capped a 16-play 56-yard drive with a Paul Rogers 25-yard field goal to put the Huskers up 3-0. Louisiana State fumbled the ball at their own 15. Two plays later, Nebraska running back Joe Orduna scored from 3-yards out with 2:06 on the opening quarter clock.

"LSU, I believe, was ranked No. 1 in the nation on defense. They had a really tough defense. In fact, I don't think they had allowed a rushing touchdown all year."

The defensive struggle mounted through the second period as both teams exchanged punts. But with 49 seconds before halftime, LSU got on the board with a 36-yard Mark Lumpkin field goal.

Louisiana State, still sailing on pre-intermission momentum, scored early in the second half. The Tigers cut Nebraska's lead to five with a Lumpkin field goal with 11:49 left in the third to cap an 80-yard drive. LSU took a 12-10 lead on the final play of the quarter when Tiger quarterback Buddy Lee hit split end Al Coffee with a 31-yard touchdown.

"They were really tough. They went ahead of us 12-10 in the fourth quarter. After they kicked off to us, we went 67 yards to get the go-ahead touchdown."

Nebraska's offense responded confidently following the lead change with a nearly eight minute 14-play touchdown drive. The series, though emotionally exhilarating, was extremely physically demanding, Newton described.

"I loved it. When I was in the huddle, I would try to communicate confidence to the other linemen and to Jerry [Tagge] and Jeff [Kinney]. I wanted that backfield to feel confident in our offensive line that the holes were going to be there–that we would open them up for them, and also that Jerry would have time to pass the ball.

"Anybody that knows anything about football, they know that the most important unit on that football team is going to be the offensive line. Because, unless that unit is a tough, hard-nosed unit, you're not going to win football games. They have to be the leaders on the football team. They're the ones that pave the way to win football games. As an offensive linemen I always tried to exude confidence to my teammates.

"In that drive, everything, the national championship was on the line and we had to get the ball in there and just give it 130 percent every play and block our hearts out. I believe that the offense got that ball in there because they played with their hearts. Our heart was in that drive. Our whole season was hanging on this fourth quarter against LSU and we had to get the job done."

It was third down and the end zone was 36 inches away. With 6:10 remaining in the fourth quarter, NU quarterback Jerry Tagge kept the ball and dove over the middle of the pile. He stretched across the goal line for the score. Nebraska led 17-12.

"It was just a quarterback sneak. The offensive line had a wedge block in a V [formation], as in a victory manner. I just remember, I was on the ground, it was hot, it was sweaty, we were all dirty, it had been a really tough game. And I just remember looking up at Jerry stretching that ball over the goal line. I remember seeing the ref putting his hands up. And I just thank God that we got it done."

The game continued to be a defensive struggle as it had been all evening. The final quarter saw four turnovers between both teams. With just under a minute remaining, LSU recovered a fumble by NU signal caller Jerry Tagge at the Tiger 40-yard line. But on the following play, Nebraska weakside linebacker Bob Terrio intercepted a pass at the Husker 38. The Huskers ran out the clock to preserve their first national championship with a 17-12 final score. With the victory, the 11-0-1 Cornhuskers vaulted to No. 1 in the Associated Press poll ahead of Notre Dame and Texas. In the United Press International poll, Texas remained No. 1 followed by Ohio State and Nebraska as the rankings were final at the conclusion of the regular season.

That spring, the California native continued his life on the gridiron as a third-round draft pick by the Chicago Bears. His 1971 season in the windy city marked the beginning of a professional career that spanned over a decade. Newton spent his first five seasons with the Bears, then five with the Seattle Seahawks between 1976 and 1982, and a portion of the 1983 season with the Boston Breakers of the now defunct United States Football League. While in Chicago, Newton said he attended pre-game chapel services, but never made Christianity a significant part of his life. His marriage ended in divorce that first season as he continued in substance abuse.

Though the fierce competitor and former All-American spent a lengthy stay in the NFL, Newton said he never reached his potential as a lineman. He described how, early in his career, a football card described him as having all-pro ability.

"On the back of that bubble gum card, it said, 'Bob Newton has the potential to be an all-pro offensive lineman. All he needs is some experience.'

"Well, I never reached that potential. It was a direct of result of my use of alcohol, marijuana, and cocaine. So, even though I played a long time, eleven years, I never played up to my potential because of my chemical dependency."

Newton consumed alcohol with reckless abandonment during his professional football years. He admitted to foolishly taking his life into his hands more than once. Several times he drove his car severely intoxicated. And while visiting in Hawaii in Jan. 1977 he even attempted to surf while drunk.

"It's by God's grace that I'm still alive. I'm grateful. I drove my car several times, severely intoxicated. I was in a near drowning incident in Hawaii in 1977. I was really hung over and I went out and tried body surfing. I got caught in a tide and I was going out to sea. God gave me the strength to hang in there and I finally got back to shore. That was a real near death situation. There have been several drinking occasions where I have been in dangerous situations, whether in driving my car or getting in fights or other instances like that."

His lifestyle sharply contrasted that of two close friends and Seattle teammates—quarterback Jim Zorn and wide receiver Steve Largent. During his tenure with the Seahawks, Fig said those two Christian athletes lived and shared their faith with him consistently. During his period with the Seahawks he never fully took their message to heart, yet he respected their commitment and enjoyed their friendship.

Newton's stay in Seattle was severed in January 1983 following a DWI charge. He then signed with the Boston Breakers of the newly formed USFL. But his football career would come to an end before the season began.

"During training camp my intoxication caused me to miss practice. I told them I would quit drinking on my own, which was always the great alibi. I was cut from the Boston Breakers.

"My coach, Dick Coury, said, and I'll never forget it, 'Unless you get some help for your drinking problem, you're going to end up on skid row.'"

Newton heeded Coury's advice and entered an Alcoholics Anonymous treatment center in Monroe, Washington on July 12, 1983.

"I was in there 28 days. One of the steps of the 12-step program to help you recover from alcoholism is that you have to turn your life and your will over to the care of God. So that started my path back to the Lord. Getting the alcohol and the other drugs out of me and getting my head cleared up. I saw that I had to replace this lifestyle with the Lord. There was a void I had tried to fill up with booze, drugs, and football. I had to fill that up with my relationship with the Lord.

"I ended up eating with the pigs like the prodigal son before I finally came to my senses. The drinking and alcoholism is very powerful. I had a deep relationship with that and it kept me from growing spiritually."

With his sobriety treatment behind him, the Big Fig returned to his alma mater and earned a bachelor's degree. He also served one year under Coach Osborne as a graduate assistant.

"I was one of the first pros to come back and get his degree. Coach Osborne was real proud of that. In fact, he had a picture of me on his desk for a long time. It was of me getting my diploma."

Newton attributed his ability to remain sober and reclaim the direction of his life to his faith in God.

"For me to remain sober and stay off alcohol and other drugs has been dependent on my relationship with the Lord. It's through prayer and asking Him to keep me sober one day at a time. He has used me in a lot of different ways to help people become more aware of alcohol and other drug problems in our society. I have spoken to hundreds of high schools and middles schools over the last 10 years. I have spoken to thousands of college athletes. I have spoken to professional athletes and just a number of people. And hopefully I've been planting seeds about the dangers of using alcohol and other drugs. I cannot tell you how grateful I am to the Lord that I don't have to drink today or use another drug. I thank Him every night before I go to bed. I thank God every day for my sobriety. I think God is using me in that way. Coach Osborne has brought me back several times to speak to the team about alcohol and drugs. He's been real supportive."

Drug and alcohol rehabilitation counseling was far from his original thoughts when pondering life after football. Fig had planned on going into real estate. But in 1986 a position opened up at the center where he was once treated. Seeing the opportunities there proved to be compelling. He could work with the staff that had helped change his life and he had a chance to help others in a similar need.

Over the years part of his mission has been to build a heightened awareness on the dangers of substance abuse. His job titles and responsibilities have been many within the Seattle area. At the Sundown M Ranch, an in-patient alcoholic treatment center for adults and adolescents, he has served as the athletic programs coordinator. He also works for Olympic Counseling Services, an adolescent out-patient treatment center. And he has remained near football as a consultant for the Seattle Seahawks' alcohol and drug treatment program. The former collegiate All-American has also worked to impact lives outside the treatment centers as a high school football coach.

Newton has seen people of all ages fall into harmful addictions. He explained how those dependencies have sadly been socially acceptable among athletes.

"In the Seattle area, I was one of the few athletes speaking out. I really felt that there was so much ignorance in our society about alcoholism and other drugs. And I wanted to speak out against that ignorance. I stressed that alcoholism is an affliction that people need help for. That was one of my big missions and still is. Back in the 1970s and early '80s there wasn't much awareness on how to help some one with an alcohol or drug problem. There really wasn't an awareness. Drinking in the NFL was socially acceptable."

As Newton continued to share his message of freedom from substance abuse, his old friend and former teammate, Steve Largent contacted him and asked him to attend a Christian conference in Sacramento, Calif. At that meeting, in 1988, Newton said he recommitted his life to the Lord.

"I started that process that began in Lincoln in 1970. When I was going through the 12-step program, they pointed me to the Lord. I kept searching and was seeking a relationship with the Lord. I really believe God saved me in Lincoln, Neb. in 1970. But I didn't change. I had left him like the prodigal son. But there I renewed my relationship to the Lord.

"I look at Christian guys like Steve Largent, who was a phenomenal football player, and the Lord was the first priority in his life. Steve has been a personal friend since 1976, he's been a tremendous influence in my life. He planted seeds, he wasn't overbearing. He leads by example and I admired him for that. He definitely shared Jesus with me. When he sent me to that professional athletes seminar, that was the most defining moment in my Christian life."

Formerly chemically dependent, Newton's stressed his reliance on God as his source of hope and strength.

"I think Coach Osborne puts it best, when he says that you have to put the Lord as your first priority in life whatever job you have; no matter what career you choose. In my case, I put football and the use of alcohol and other drugs first in my life. And they eventually let me down. But the Lord will always be there for you and He doesn't leave you."

The Latter 1970s

Establishing the Osborne era

During these years, Coach Tom Osborne's teams flawlessly carried the baton of excellence in transition from the Devaney era with annual top-10 finishes and bowl trips.

For 1978 All-American defensive end George Andrews, his college days were a period to share his faith.

"The highlight of my Nebraska career came when we beat Oklahoma for the first time in years. I remember after the game an announcer asked me if this was the greatest moment of my life. And I was able to share that it wasn't. It was a neat time to share my faith."

For 1979 All-American Junior Miller, one of the school's greatest tight ends of all time, it was a period of carousing and alcoholism that he said might have ended in suicide had he not asked God to enter his life.

"I truly became a born-again person, because I know that Junior Miller didn't change himself," he said. "I know God changed me. A lot of my friends have met me and talked to me since. [And] I'm not the same guy. A lot of them notice it right away–the minute they see me, even before I open my mouth."

Though Andrews and Miller lived opposite lifestyles in college, they now share a common bond in Christ.

George Andrews

Moments

#96

The brightest moment of his athletic career has continued to loom within the memories of former All-American defensive end George Andrews. It was November 11, 1978.

Fourth-ranked Nebraska had just pulled the unbelievable on their home field with a 17-14 win over No. 1 Oklahoma. The Cornhuskers had not beaten the Sooners since the '71 Game of the Century in Norman. But this team was on a mission and was riding a nine-game winning streak after falling to then top-rated Alabama in the season opener at Birmingham. The senior defensive lineman finished the game with seven tackles, including two for 16 yards in losses.

Reporters flanked the team's defensive captain following the upset. One television journalist asked the 6-foot-4-inch, 225-pound All-American what the victory meant to him.

"An announcer asked me after the game, 'Is this the greatest day in your life?'

"And I was able to share that it wasn't, because it would pass," Andrews reflected. "But I said that I had a relationship that would last for eternity. It was a special opportunity to share my faith."

Andrews said the greatest event of his life took place when he was a college freshman. In March 1975, Andrews prayed in his dormitory room to receive Christ as Savior. The example of his Christian roommate, quarterback Tom Sorley of Big Springs, Texas, had made a profound impact upon his life.

"Tom was the first person that I had been close to that was a born-again Christian. And when I went to Lincoln and was on my own for the first time, I just noticed that Tom was able to stand up to peer pressure. When the guys went out at night to party, he would always have a reason not to go. He just knew that was something he didn't want to be involved in. And I respected that, because I wasn't able to take that stand. I wanted to be accepted by the group. And something that was a dream of every Nebraska player to have was a scholarship. And I realized that it wasn't fulfilling. I just saw that things don't fill that void. Christ is the answer. It was through his example and being convicted of my sin in those areas that God worked in my heart. And it was through talking with him at night and going through different situations that really revealed that I didn't know Christ in a personal way."

But Tom Sorley's words and lifestyle were nothing new to the Omaha Burke graduate. The defensive lineman was raised by God-fearing parents, he attended church regularly, and learned right from wrong. Though their Christian example was exceptional to him, he said they were private about discussing their faith. He heard the gospel message twice in high school—from a basketball coach and also from a teammate.

"My coach was the first person that ever tried to share Christ with me from a personal standpoint, but I wasn't interested at that point."

His friend offered him a tract, that Andrews said, did spark some interest. Nevertheless, he laid those thoughts aside.

As a senior the Burke High standout athlete received a scholarship offer from Nebraska during December 1973.

"For my recruiting trip, I drove down in my Volkswagen bug," Andrews chuckled in remembrance. "There wasn't much to it."

Following his conversion at the university, Andrews made his faith a viable part of his everyday life at a time when he said it was not very fashionable for athletes to call themselves Christians. He joined various Christian fellowship groups and Bible studies to learn and find fellowship.

"Immediately I noticed that my language cleared up. I did use profanity and I wanted to stop that. And I began to have a desire to be around other Christians."

But his freshman roommate was married shortly after their first year and the defensive lineman said he found himself alone occasionally after games.

"It was hard because you didn't have a lot of people to hang out with. And guys would go out to the bars after the game. So, there were some lonely times from that standpoint. But that's just part of having a Christian walk."

He later became close friends with defensive end Gordon Thiessen and defensive back Craig Bohl [current UNL inside linebackers coach].

"During my junior and senior year we would meet and have a Bible study. That was the beginning of any kind of Bible study on the team back then."

As fellow senior captains, he and Sorley travelled the state speaking at several churches for six straight weeks.

"I had a lot of chances to share my testimony. I think God gives us all a platform in some way. And when people give you the opportunity to share your faith, I think we need to take advantage of that. We need to look for those opportunities."

On the field, the 1978 Cornhuskers entered the season with a dream of winning coach Tom Osborne's first Big Eight Championship. When the Sooners appeared in Lincoln that November, emotions were high as well as the stakes. A victory meant a possible road to the national championship for either team.

Oklahoma scored first as 1978 Heisman Trophy running back Billy Sims broke free for a 44-yard touchdown with 8:09 to go in the opening quarter. Nebraska tied up the game at 7-7 in the second period as the battle ensued. Entering the final quarter, the game was even at 14 apiece. But the Huskers would take the lead for good as Nebraska kicker Billy Todd booted a 24-yard field goal with 11:51 remaining. The rival teams then exchanged scoreless drives. With 6:11 remaining, Oklahoma took over the ball at their own 47. Nearly three minutes later, the Sooners faced third-and-six at the Nebraska 20. The play went to the nation's leading Heisman candidate. Sims, eyeing the end zone, broke free for the first down and gained 17 yards–but coughed up the ball at the Nebraska three as Husker defender Jim Pillen recovered. The turnover was Oklahoma's sixth of the afternoon. With 3:27 remaining, Nebraska's offense gained three more first downs and ran out the clock to preserve a 17-14 win.

"That was a fantastic team they had. If we had played them nine out of ten times they would have probably beat us. It was a thrill to be part of a senior class that had finally beat Oklahoma. We were going to the Orange Bowl for the first time."

But his team's emotional high following the upset was not enough to carry them past un-ranked Missouri the following week in Lincoln. With 75,850 fans at Memorial Stadium, No. 2 Nebraska dropped a 31-24 contest to the Tigers. Visions of a national championship matchup were lost.

"That was the lowest point of my Nebraska career. Our entire team was emotionally flat. We just couldn't get up for it emotionally. You're No. 2 and you have a chance to go for No. 1 if you win. But it just wasn't our day. It's not easy in sports to go from an extreme high to an extreme low. They had a good team and they played a good game."

With the loss, the Nebraska and Oklahoma tied for the conference championship. And to the Huskers' dismay, there would be a rematch in the Jan. 1, 1979 Orange Bowl.

"After the game we heard we had to play Oklahoma in the Orange Bowl. And that was another blow!" Andrews chuckled. "There was not a lot of excitement, obviously, just having played them the week before. It was great to be going to the Orange Bowl. I felt a little bit cheated. But if you thought about it, they were a good pick for the [Orange Bowl] committee to make."

In Miami, sixth-ranked Nebraska went into the locker room down by seven points. But a 17-point Sooner run in the third quarter would prove insurmountable as Oklahoma claimed a 31-24 victory. The Huskers ended the season ranked eighth as their rival finished at No. 3.

That spring, Andrews joined the Los Angeles Rams as a linebacker after being chosen as the 19th overall pick in the first round of the NFL draft. There on the west coast he was reunited with Nebraska's 1976 All-American quarterback, Vince Ferragamo.

"During my freshman year in the dormitory, Vince happened to live just two doors down from me," Andrews grinned in recollection. "I got to know him then. We became friends over the years. So it was fun to go there [to Los Angeles]. He did a good job that year."

The 1979 Rams recorded only nine wins during the regular season, yet put themselves into position for a run at the post-season. During the playoffs, Los Angeles edged the Super Bowl XII champion Dallas Cowboys 21-19 in Texas. One week later, they only needed nine points to shut out Tampa Bay on the road in the NFC Championship game. On Jan. 20, 1980 in Super Bowl XIV, they faced the three-time defending Super Bowl Champion Pittsburgh Steelers at Pasadena's Rose Bowl. In retrospect, the challenge for the Ram's was evident, attempt to knock off one of the NFL's greatest dynasties of all time.

"It was fun just playing against people or with people you had heard of as house-hold names. We played against guys like Terry Bradshaw, Franco Harris, and Lynn Swann. You don't realize until it's over how good they were. That was their fourth championship. What they accomplished was really amazing.

"It was just amazing as a rookie to be able to go to the Super Bowl. The Rams had never been there. You don't really realize how hard sometimes it is to get there when you are a rookie. I just remember that it was the ultimate time in my sports career to be able participate in that."

The Omaha native recalled his own plays within the game.

"The only time I was involved was during an onside kick. They pooched the kick and I was able to catch it and run with it."

In the end, Pittsburgh claimed their fourth title in six years with a 31-19 victory over Los Angeles.

In spite of the loss, Andrews enjoyed the opportunity. And yet, he admitted to a general sense of unfulfillment.

"Although we lost, I remember saying to myself, 'Is that all there is?' I believe all of us go through life unsatisfied with our accomplishments, unless we understand that glorifying God is our main purpose in life."

Circumstances can be unfulfilling no matter how glorious, he surmised.

Andrews played his final game in 1985. Following two knee reconstructions in a nine-month period, injuries forced him to retire during summer training camp prior to the 1986 season. The period of transition from the game he loved and moving into the business world was relatively frustrating for him, he said. But the most difficult moments of Andrews life came between May and September of 1994.

During that late spring, George lost his father-in-law to cancer. Approximately four months later, his father passed away due to a complication of illnesses that culminated over a five-year period. In July, between those deaths, their new-born son would spend two weeks in intensive care.

"My wife, toward the end of her pregnancy, didn't feel our son Ryan moving. We went in and he was strangling himself to death by the umbilical cord. And they did an emergency Caesarean section and got him out just in time. And the next couple weeks, it could have gone either way. But I really believe God worked and healed him and he's doing great today.

"It was a time when I learned that sometimes we don't have the strength to go on within ourselves. And just at the right time, God would send a few of my friends over to the hospital to visit. And I would draw strength from them and their prayers."

Those four months and the following were extremely painful and difficult. Yet, it was truly a time of character growth, he said.

"That was just a condensed period of going through a lot of different things where you see that your faith is real and you cling to God. It was really a time where you feel almost like you're in a dark tunnel. You see how little control you have over your own life. But God teaches you through that to have hope in Him and trust Him. And you don't know how it's going to come out, but He's still good no matter what happens. When it's all breaking loose around you, He's still there no matter what. You learn to walk by faith and not by sight."

In light of those hardships, Andrews said he found encouragement from Philippians 1:6, "Being confident of this, that He who began a good work in you will carry it on to completion until the day of Christ Jesus." (NIV)

"I like that verse because it means that God has started a work in me and I am involved in that," he explained. "And He is going to make sure that I am complete. We all go through trials. And it just gives me a comfort and a hope because the Christian life is a marathon."

And that faith has enabled him to find joy and hope during both the highest and lowest moments of life.

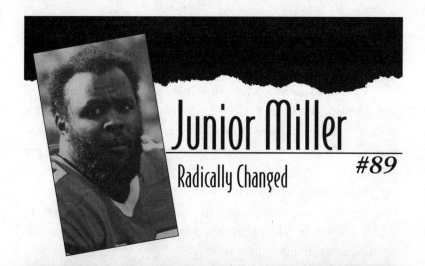

Junior Miller

Radically Changed

#89

All-American Tight End 1979,
Third Team All-American 1978,
All-Big Eight 1978-79, three-year letterman 1977-79

"I was an alcoholic," admitted former Nebraska All-American tight end Junior Miller.

"I believed in God, but I never really took time to search Him out. I thought that I was successful, but I was becoming a failure with my marriage. I was becoming a failure with professional football. And I was becoming a failure to myself, because I didn't spend any quality time with my wife or kids. I spent all my time at the lake drinking. I believe there were a lot of people praying for Junior Miller."

The hulking former Pro Bowl receiver stood on the Cornhusker sidelines during a practice. His large hands on his waist, Junior's bright friendly eyes widened as he turned to see a friend from his college days of alcohol and marijuana approach. The change in Miller's heart was evident before he said a word to the newcomer.

"Junior!" The friend exclaimed. "You changed!"

"What are you talking about?" Miller replied with a grin as he shook his hand.

"You look so... clean."

"That's the Lord!" Miller beamed sincerely.

"A lot of my old friends have met me and talked to me since," Junior reflected with a smile. "Strangely enough, they don't like being around me because I'm not the same guy. And a lot of them notice it right away–the minute they see me, even before I open my mouth."

The former tight end was born Selvia Miller [after his father] in 1957 to loving parents among a litter of seven children. Raised in Midland, Texas, he laughed in remembrance of how he obtained his permanent nickname in high school.

"I just told people to call me "Junior," because they used to call me Sylvester or Sylvia."

As a youth, Junior's Christian mother made sure the children attended church regularly. Irene Miller lived her faith, he said.

"My mom loved the Lord. I often saw her praying. She always made us go to church."

But as an adult, Miller rebelled from his upbringing. Prior to accepting Christ, Miller described himself as a self-serving alcoholic and life of the party. Personal glory and self-satisfaction consumed his heart prior to his conversion. He was a consensus All-American tight end in 1979. He played seven seasons in the NFL with Atlanta and New Orleans. Following the 1980 and '81 seasons, he was selected for the Pro Bowl. Yet one night he found himself alone in his van, parked near a lake. He was drunk and contemplating suicide.

His thoughts of personal destruction may have stemmed in part from a demonic experience he said he endured years prior. For it was that night he initially despised Christianity. As a sophomore at the university, Junior read a Gideon Bible prior to going to bed. But before he could fall asleep, Miller said a demon threatened his life if he ever read the scriptures again.

"It wasn't a dream. It happened to me. Something just jumped on me and grabbed me and pinned me to the floor."

From that moment until his conversion, Miller said he rejected Christianity. That same night, Junior explained that he slipped into a trance-like state and built an altar to satan in his apartment. His girlfriend came over the next morning and, upon seeing it, tore the shrine apart.

"Spiritual wickedness is real. I got into it and I didn't even realize what I was doing. I got attacked by a demon. I have no shadow of doubt that it was a demon."

And thus, nine years later in 1986, he sat alone at the lake. He peered at the night sky, tormented by both his thoughts and the alcohol in his system.

"My wife and I had a big argument and I was drunk. She kicked me out of the house and I ended up at Branched Oak Lake [northwest of Lincoln, Neb.]. I started to think about what I had accomplished and the things that I had done. And I started to hurt inside.

"And there was a real strong voice that came, not an audible voice, it was just a voice within inside of me. This voice was so strong that it told me to kill myself, that I was washed up and no good. And this voice got really strong and it started to hurt. And I started to cry like a little baby because I thought I was losing control of myself. And as I continued to cry, I just yelled out for Jesus. I yelled out, 'Jesus, come into my life!'

"I was sincere in my heart. And all I know is that the minute that I said those words, it was done. That was it. The battle was over. I wasn't drunk anymore. I was drunk before I said it, but as soon as I said it, I was sober. I was an alcoholic and I had been smoking six or seven packs of cigarettes a day. But I haven't had a drink since then. I haven't had a cigarette since then. I had a very filthy mouth, I can't even curse anymore. I mean, that type of language doesn't even come out of anger. I truly became a born-again person, because I know that Junior Miller didn't change himself. I know God changed me. And when He changed me, there was a love that I had toward Him. And there was a zeal to know Him more than I have ever known anything. And I just fell in love with His Word."

Following his conversion, Junior returned home that same night. His wife Carol, already a Christian, was not easily convinced of his change of heart.

"Right after I gave my life over to Christ, I was really excited and happy. I went home and told my wife. She didn't believe me at first, but after a time she believed me and my marriage got stronger."

Junior noted that it was probably a poor choice on his wife's part that she ever married the ungodly heavy drinker in the first place. However, God was gracious and caused it to work out for good, he said.

"People have asked her, 'Why did you marry Junior when he wasn't a Christian?'

"And I have always said, God has a plan. He corrected the mistakes that we made and made it better. She probably messed up when she married me, but God made it better."

Junior desired to learn more about his newly accepted faith. He sought knowledge and wisdom from scripture. But reading was a natural struggle as he had been plagued by dyslexia his entire life.

"When I was going to the University of Nebraska, I had a hard time reading. I couldn't understand anything. I would stumble over words. I used to try hard. I had tutors help me, but I couldn't do anything. But when I gave my life over to Christ, the first book I learned how to read was the Bible. Now I can read anything.

"When I gave my life over to Christ, I was so hungry for truth. I just knew that the truth was in His Word. I would stumble and really not understand what I was reading. But I would read and pray and put it down. And I would just continue to do that every day. And within two weeks, I was reading the Bible with no problem. With God all things are possible."

But life's hardships were far from over for Junior Miller. During the following months, the aging receiver found himself out of a job and in a financial strait. After accepting bad advice, he said he unknowingly made an illegal investment. The decision cost him dearly following an audit by the Internal Revenue Service.

"Financially, things got really bad. I was cut by the Saints. No one wanted me in the whole NFL. I was audited by the IRS. They hit me with interest and penalties and I ended up losing my house in Lincoln.

"It was like the world stripped Junior Miller down to bare nothing. You would think, when a person gives their life over to Christ, things get better. But they didn't. They got worse. It seemed like all hell broke out against me. But I had total faith and confidence in God. I said, 'Father God, I know you're real because I know you heard me that night I cried. Your Word says that You will never leave me nor forsake me. And He didn't. Though I lost everything, my wife stayed with me.

"People used to always say, 'Your wife married you because of your money.'

"And I can remember the day when we were flat-busted and had to get out of our house. And she looked at me and said, 'Well, Dear, I didn't marry you for your money.'

"That's a good feeling!" Junior exclaimed in reflection, as he knew they were committed to each other for better or for worse.

And through faith in God and perseverance, he was determined to overcome his adversities.

"At that time, I wasn't concerned about the debt. I wasn't concerned about the house I was losing. I was hurting to be losing everything, in a sense. For a guy who was making almost $10,000 a month and now, all of a sudden, he's digging a ditch for three dollars an hour and moving furniture, that can be painful. But I have always said, I'm an 'ol country boy, anyway, and to work, has never bothered me. I don't care how much money I personally make as long as it's legal and it's honest hard work."

Though strapped financially, in 1987, Miller said he was directed to start his current business venture.

"Miller Mailing, Inc. was given to us by the Lord. One day I was walking around the house, really sad and teary eyed. I knew we had to get out of there. I had just got fired. And the bank had told me to get out of my house. And I asked the Lord, 'what am I going to do with my life, because I don't know what to do?' It was kind of tough."

All Junior knew was that he and his wife would relocate outside Lincoln. Carol was working part-time. Miller believed God then prompted him with a plan.

"'Take what your wife is doing and sell it. And I will bless it.'" Miller described.

The prospect met with her approval, but a relative offered a differing viewpoint.

"'Junior, you don't have any money.'" Miller recalled the sincere, yet direct words. "'You lost your job. You have two used cars you just bought with bald tires on them. And you are moving 40-some miles away from Lincoln and you are talking about starting a business. Junior, you don't know the difference between faith and stupidity.'"

"You know, I could have taken that personally." Junior chuckled amiably as he recalled the friendly advice. "But I just said, 'I know the Lord told me to do this and He said He would bless it. And I believe it.'"

Miller said that relatives helped pay some of their bills and provide food during the new company's early months. The business grew rapidly during its first year. Miller Mailing, Inc. now employs 16 workers and handles business mailings, Junior said.

"The company just kind of grew within three months and we were on our own. And here we are today."

Though he has found success in his personal and business life, Miller explained how fragile life's circumstances can be. The death of three close friends within close time proximity reminded him of what is most important.

"That was devastating. Those incidents are real. And it showed me how vulnerable life really is and how we take everything for granted. We think we are going to live forever, and think about buying fancy cars and a fancy house. But we forget about the most important thing in this life, and that's living for our heavenly Father."

Periods of Junior's life testimony have been somber, indeed, but his favorite memory as a collegiate athlete was somewhat comical. It was a moment he described as uncharacteristic of coach Osborne. It was Sept. 29, 1979 with No. 18 Penn State at sixth-ranked Nebraska. In the second quarter, Nebraska trailed by a touchdown. NU quarterback Tim Hager hit the All-American tight end with a 70-yard scoring strike to tie the game at 14 en route to a 42-17 victory. The catch was Miller's second touchdown reception of the day.

"I had never seen coach Osborne get emotional. But when I scored the second touchdown against Penn State and was coming off the field, this guy ran up to me with a big 'ol smile on his face.

He put his hands up in the air and gave me a hug!" Junior roared with laughter. "I was shocked! I don't think I'll ever forget the look on Coach Osborne's face."

Perhaps Nebraska's best-ever tight end, Miller could have played collegiate basketball. The 6-foot-4 receiver said he tried out for Joe Cipriano's cage squad and had the opportunity to start. He stayed solely with football, however, citing that he had a better chance at making the pros on the gridiron.

Miller played for a 1978 Nebraska team that was coach Tom Osborne's first to beat Oklahoma. The fourth-ranked Cornhuskers upset the No. 1 Sooners 17-14 in Lincoln only to fall to unranked Missouri a week later at home. But Junior says that lone win over Oklahoma has hardly stood as a great personal memory as the two teams rematched in the Orange Bowl. The Sooners came out on top, 31-24.

"That was a good victory for us because we hadn't beaten them in a long time. But it took the luster off that year because we didn't accomplish that year what we wanted because Missouri spoiled the party the following week. And then we had to play Oklahoma again and that killed it even more so."

Yes, Miller's life, both on and off the field, has truly been one marked by highs and lows. But through his faith in God, he said he has found strength to persevere.

"All things are possible for those who believe," he smiled.

The Early 1980s

Potent offenses and title contenders

During the 1981-83 seasons, three straight Nebraska teams came within a whisker of glory in their pursuit of a national championship. Though each squad came up short on the scoreboard, they were champions because of their perseverance.

Irving Fryar, a 1983 All-American wingback and member of the Scoring Explosion offense related how God gave him hope and forgiveness after living a life of violence and substance abuse.

"I was basically tired of being sick and tired. The Lord was tugging at my heart and I knew I had to do something about it. I would have probably wound up going down the drain.

"I finally got enough courage to say, 'God, I know I messed up. You see all and You know all. God, if you can find it in Your heart to forgive me, have Your way with me.'

"And before I could even finish praying that prayer, God saved me. He changed my life."

For three-time All-Big Eight quarterback Turner Gill, it was an enjoyable era, yet, ultimately it left him empty.

"I still needed something more, but I didn't know what it was. That's when I shared my feelings and [a teammate] shared with me about Christ. 'Here's what you need.'"

Meanwhile, split end Todd Brown and defensive end Bill Weber found their collegiate years as foundational in their spiritual lives.

On the field, each of these men pushed themselves to be the best. But only because of their faith in Christ, they are truly complete.

Turner Gill

Confident Option Specialist #12

Quarterbacks coach 1992-present,
Fourth in 1983 Heisman Trophy balloting,
Second team All-America quarterback 1983,
All-Big Eight 1981-83, NU offensive captain 1983,
three year letterman 1981-83

He grew up a Sooner fan.

It was a cold, wet afternoon in Norman's Memorial Stadium, and Nebraska quarterback Turner Gill simply wanted to take it all in. The top-ranked Huskers just finished a perfect 1983 season with a narrow 28-21 road win over Oklahoma, and Turner stood one game away from a dream. Sooner coach Barry Switzer extended a congratulatory hand and extolled him for a phenomenal season and college career. As Switzer made his way to his team's locker room, Turner may have reflected momentarily on his youth—when he cheered for the Big Red of the South.

It was fall 1979 in Fort Worth, Texas and baseball was his first love. He was an all-state quarterback at Arlington Heights High School and was one of the top football prospects in the country. He would also be selected in the second round of the free-agent draft by the Chicago White Sox that spring. Several recruiters desired him to play receiver or defensive back at their school, but he wanted to direct a top program's offense and play on the diamond as well. His top choices came down to the campuses of Norman, Oklahoma and Lincoln, Nebraska.

Turner's final decision rested on the reputation of one man– Tom Osborne.

"The biggest factor was Tom Osborne," Turner explained. "I remember people telling me I could trust his word. There's no doubt he was the reason [I went to Nebraska], because all indications pointed me toward Oklahoma. I grew up saying, 'if I ever get an opportunity for a scholarship, I want to go to Oklahoma.'"

Not a fan of the Lone Star State's collegiate football program, Turner had always been fascinated by the Oklahoma-Texas rivalry. Ironically, the Sooner convert signed with Oklahoma's other major foe.

"I really believed that he [Osborne] was going to give me an opportunity to play football, play quarterback, and then play baseball."

Gill played junior varsity ball his first year as a Husker. He entered his sophomore 1981 season as the No. 3 quarterback behind senior Mark Mauer and junior Nate Mason. But fearing that he might not see significant playing time, Gill considered quitting at the season's end to focus strictly on baseball.

"Deep down inside, I was thinking that this was going to be my last year in football and I'd just play baseball. I would finish out the season, work hard in practice, and just see what happens."

His moment of opportunity came on October 3, 1981. Mason was out with a broken ankle and Mauer was having an off day against Auburn. Osborne let the sophomore play in the second quarter and start the second half.

"[Going into halftime] It was tied 3-3. We were already one-and-two and looking like we were going to be one-and-three."

Gill piloted the Huskers past Auburn 17-3 and eventually won

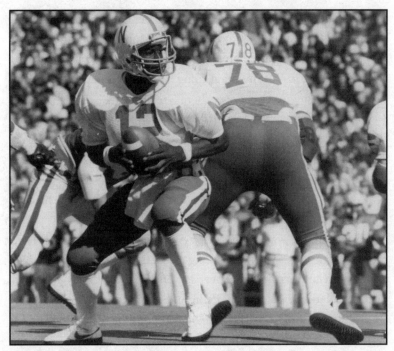

the starting job for good. He led the Huskers to six straight wins before suffering nerve damage in his lower right leg against Iowa State. The injury sidelined him for the remainder of his sophomore season.

"I really don't know of a specific play or a specific hit when it [the injury] actually happened. I think it was just probably over a period of time that it came about."

Turner endured two surgeries and a lengthy rehabilitation process before feeling any more physical contact. He underwent his first operation late following the Iowa State contest. His second took place in mid-December.

"I was on crutches for a while, then they made a special brace. It was a shoe that had a brace attached to my leg. I had to wrap it around my calf area and keep my foot up. I didn't have any movement in that for five months. It was a long process."

On January 1, Gill observed from the bench as Nebraska fell to Clemson 22-15 in the National Championship Orange Bowl.

"I was watching the game from the sidelines. It was tough, no question about it. But my main thing was to try to keep the spirits up on the team and encourage them."

Turner's road back began in mid-March when he found he could move his big toe for the first time since the injury. Weeks passed as the flexibility extended through the remainder of his foot and lower leg.

When he could tread freely again, the signal caller ran through spring football drills, but avoided any contact.

Next fall, he was ready to play again. Gill directed the 1982 Huskers to a 12-1 season, including a 21-20 Orange Bowl win over Louisiana State and a controversial 27-24 regular season loss to eventual National Champion Penn State.

But in the spring of 1983, Gill again considered playing on the diamond full-time.

"That spring there was a possibility that I would leave and enter the professional baseball draft. But I really enjoyed the experience of college football. I was the starter and we had a great team coming back. We definitely had a legitimate opportunity to be national champions.

"I also felt that the overriding factor was my education. I felt that if I left at the end of my junior year and played pro baseball, I would probably never get my degree. That was one reason I didn't go [play pro baseball] right out of high school, because I wanted to get a degree to have something to fall back on."

With a shot at the title and the opportunity to extend his education, Gill elected to remain in Lincoln and placed baseball on the backburner.

Then came the 1983 Scoring Explosion. The '83 Husker offense outscored regular season opponents by an average score of 52-to-16–until Miami.

The 1983 Huskers, then touted by some sports analysts as one of the greatest teams ever, found themselves trailing freshman quarterback Bernie Kosar's Hurricanes 17-0 in the first quarter of the Jan. 2, 1984 National Championship Orange Bowl.

"I was a little upset, maybe a little shocked, that we were behind by 17 points. But still, deep down inside, I felt we were going to win the ball game."

Nebraska got on the board midway through the second quarter when All-American offensive guard Dean Steinkuler cruised 19 yards for a touchdown on a fumblerooski play.

The Huskers tied the score at 17 early in the third quarter on a Scott Livingston 34-yard field goal, but Alonzo Highsmith and Albert Bently added two more TDs for the Canes only short minutes later.

National title hopes darkened on Nebraska's next series when Heisman Trophy winner Mike Rozier was sidelined with a badly bruised ankle, but junior I-back Jeff Smith came in to rush for 99 yards.

Smith added a 1-yard fourth quarter touchdown to his stats with 6:55 remaining.

Trailing 24-to-31 with barely a minute to play, the Big Red faced fourth and eight at the Miami 24.

Turner knew it was not over.

"In the huddle I was reminding the players, 'When we score, don't get too excited because we are going to go for two points [on the conversion]. I don't want us to get a five-yard penalty for delay of game. When we score, don't celebrate too much, because we have to get in the huddle and get ready to go for two points.'

"It was fourth and eight. We called a play to [All-American wingback] Irving [Fryar]. It was a slant pattern. If he's not open, then I run the option. It was a do or die deal."

Ball in hand, Turner looked for Irving and opted to keep it. Shy of the first down marker, Gill pitched to the trailing back, Smith. Smith pounded his way to the end zone for a 24-yard score.

Forty-eight seconds remained. Turner huddled the offense together. Gill looked to the sideline as Osborne flashed the two-point play sign.

The Scoring explosion offense broke huddle and lined up for their final scoring attempt.

The snap.

Fryar sped out as a decoy receiver.

Jeff Smith had a step on defender strong safety Ken Calhoun at the goal line. Gill fired to the Husker I-back, but the ball never reached his hands as Calhoun reached and deflected it.

"I tried to get the ball to Jeff Smith, but it got tipped. The ball hit him in the chest and it bounced up—an incompletion. That's it!

"I came off the field in tears and in a sense of disbelief. We had time for the onside kick. I stood beside coach Tom Osborne, still believing, but crying.

"But any opportunities disappeared when Miami recovered the onside kick. I went into a daze. I didn't hear or see anything. I looked out on the field in disbelief that we didn't do it. It was tough after that game to go on."

The resilient athlete did move on. For Turner, the sting from the national loss lasted momentarily. Yet, he sensed a burning unfulfillment. In his heart lay a chasm. It was a void far deeper than the pain felt that January night in Miami.

Turner knew he had played to the best of his ability in the Orange Bowl. and throughout his collegiate athletic career. He found some peace in that. He had accomplished great things on the gridiron and he bore a future in the pros, yet he was admittedly unhappy. It was disenchanting.

Opting to ignore those feelings, the mobile quarterback continued his athletic endeavors north of the border with the Canadian

Football League. As a Montreal Concorde, he was reunited with a Cornhusker teammate, split end Todd Brown. The two grew close.

During Gill's second season, Brown was sidelined with a broken leg. Though injured, the receiver's vigor was not abated.

"He was still so inspired and just so alive," Turner smiled to himself. "It was like he was still playing. He was an inspiration to me.

"I had the money and the fame and I still needed something more, but I didn't know what it was. That's when I shared my feelings with him and he shared with me about Christ. 'Here's what you need.'"

He pondered Todd's words. A short time passed. In December 1985 Turner listened to a speaker at a Christian hockey ministry event. He left the meeting knowing what he should do.

"That night I went home and was with my wife and [said], 'Hey, I need the Lord in my life.' I got down on my knees and asked Christ to come into my life.

"I called him [Todd Brown] that next morning and told him about it. He was just ecstatic.

"I can really feel why everybody before me, that were Christians, were trying to get me to know Christ. Because once you know Christ, you hate to see other people not having the same enthusiasm in knowing that the Lord is always going to be there."

But the gospel message was not unfamiliar to Turner. Until he spent time with Brown in the CFL, he avoided anything that seemed too religious. As a child, his Christian mother took he and his two sisters to church regularly. But young Turner continually snuck out of Sunday school when mom was not around.

Even following his leg injury as a sophomore, a doctor counselled him to pray concerning his health.

"He just told me, 'Turner, there's a 50-50 chance that it [full recovery] may come back. The only way that you're going to come back is by prayer and your hard work in rehabilitation.'"

Gill said that the doctor's words were thought provoking for him. "It touched me. This doctor is supposed to heal me and he told me to pray about it. It really shocked me. I was thinking that he was going to heal me and he started talking about prayer and God. That stunned me a little bit. We think that doctors are supposed to heal us and not Someone else. It was touching, but I still had a pretty hard heart toward God."

Turner did not soften his spirit until he realized the temporal things of earth could not bring him lasting happiness.

"I saw that God was using other people to get me to know Christ and I kind of had a hard heart for so long. It wasn't something just traumatic that hit for me to get to know Christ. I did have that injury early on [as a sophomore at Nebraska], but that still didn't open my heart. And it took me even longer than that to have an open mind and accept Christ."

As a new believer, Turner still faced struggles. His pro football career was cut short after he endured three concussions during his second season. Following medical tests and physicals, two separate doctors would not grant him clearance to play on the gridiron.

"Of course, that hurt. It ended my career as a football player. I had to decide what I would end up doing. I just figured that the Lord had another plan for me. I accepted that it was time to move on to something else in my life."

Something else turned out to be his first love in athletics.

"I had always loved baseball, and people were interested in me in baseball. My agent thought that I should at least give it a shot. So, we called to see if there were any teams interested, and there were."

From 1986 through 1988, he played in the Cleveland and Detroit minor league systems before choosing to return to the football sidelines, as a coach.

In 1990 he served as a volunteer assistant at North Texas and completed his psychology degree. Gill came back to Nebraska that same year as a graduate assistant and then moved to Southern Methodist for the 1991 season.

In 1992 he returned to his alma mater as a full-time assistant, coaching quarterbacks.

For the time being, he indicated contentment with his position. His goals lie not in moving up the ladder, but in the process of molding young players into educated men of character.

"The reason why I am a coach is that I want to be able to influence young people. Hopefully I can influence them for Christ. Secondly, when all is said and done, is that they have an education. I really don't have a strong goal to be a head coach. That's really not why I'm in coaching. If it happens, great, if it doesn't, that's also great, too."

Irving Fryar

Rebel to Reverend

#27

*All-American and
All-Big Eight wingback 1983,
three-year letterman 1981-83*

Irving Fryar was born between his sisters Faith and Hope amidst gang violence in the suburbs of southwest New Jersey. He ignored the instruction of his Christian mother and lived the neighborhood code. The blue chip defensive back of Rancocas Valley Regional High patterned his off-field lifestyle after surrounding adult male figures.

"They had been through some things in their lives–involved with drugs, different marriages, a whole lot of chaos in their life. Those were the things that I saw. Those were the things that I was around. There was just the absence of a role model early in my life."

Yet, there was one godly man he quietly looked up to, his uncle Arnold Oakman.

"He didn't do anything so special, he was just a man who had a wife and two children who cared and took care of his wife and children. He was a family man who sacrificed for his family. He was just there for everybody. There was a foundation. He was solid. He was mature. He was a leader. I always liked that in him. I always looked up to him. Even to this day, he is the person that I try to be like."

Young Fryar left those aspirations unpursued. Yet the man's example remained etched within the back of his mind.

"As I became a teenager I started trying to become my own person, and do my own thing—not so much being influenced by older people. I was trying to figure out my own identity. I was in a gang. I was with a group of guys that were into creating chaos. We robbed and we stole and we fought and we did drugs and drank and all the things that a gang does. I started when I was 13. We called ourselves 'G-Town', because it was Ghetto town. We fought against gangs in other towns. We didn't do guns and those types of things. We fought with our hands. Every now and then someone would bring out a knife or a baseball bat or something like that."

Irving recalled his last gang fight. It was his senior year in high school. An opposing gang member wrongly accused him of stealing his girl and they were to meet at a local pizza parlor.

"They drove up in their cars and took their bats and knives out. I guess there were about 30 or 40 of them and there were about eight of us. And we looked at each other and said, 'Look, we can run or we can throw down and if we get beat, we're all going to get beat together.' And we said, 'We'll just have to get beat together.'"

But the opposing gang member challenged Irving one-on-one.

"Then this guy punched me in the face. So I took my jacket off and while they were still talking, I reached across and hit him. And we began to fight. And as we were fighting, we swung each other through this big picture window of the pizza parlor. And it was like I was out for a second and woke up. He was laying next to me and I was laying on the pallet behind the counter in the pizza parlor. And he jumped up and ran back through the window and one of my friends had a knife and cut him in the side. And I had a big gouge in my head from going through the window. And I jumped

out through the window and we got in our cars and they got in their cars and sped off.

"And that was the last time I fought with a gang because I could have wound up in the hospital. In fact, he wound up in the hospital. He had to get 15-to-20 stitches. I didn't go the hospital. In fact, I should have got stitches. I still have the mark in my forehead. I should have probably had about three or four stitches in my head."

Irving had hoped to keep the brawl secret from his temporarily ill mother, who was receiving hospital care. But the opposing gang member was treated in the same institution where his mother resided. And word got around.

"My mother found out about it somehow, someway. And she explained to me that I can't do those type of things, especially with her being sick. I could have wound up next to her. She was just giving me the worst case scenario of what could have happened that night."

Though it did not happen and he permanently abandoned the gangs to attend the University of Nebraska in the fall, the strife remained in his heart. The relatively slow pace of the midwestern town was a culture shock, but it was therapeutic. The quiet head coach who had recruited him offered a sense of stability that the young man of Mount Holly, N.J. appreciated.

"I was able to get out of that atmosphere when I went to college. It was pretty tough. It was total culture shock. It was totally different than I was used to.

"In fact, I came to Nebraska because of coach Osborne and how he treated me. He was very true when all the other coaches were promising me the world and doing all kinds of crazy stuff and doing all kinds of fast talking and all that stuff. I knew if something went wrong when I was way out here in Nebraska, I could go to Tom and tell him what's wrong and he would help me. [Assistant coach Frank] Solich was true, too. He was actually the one who was doing the recruiting. He was down to earth when he talked and made sense. When he talked, he was kind of the same as Osborne. And I respected what he said. I felt like I could believe what he said. That's why I came out to Nebraska."

Ironically, Irving labeled his recruiting visit to the Cornhusker state as his worst.

"I came here on a Monday and a Tuesday and it was a blizzard. I didn't do anything. I mean some of the recruiting trips I went on, I had a blast. It was a weekend. I was partying and hanging out with the fellas and hanging out with the girls and had a great time on my recruiting trip. And this was my worst recruiting trip. But I just really wanted to come."

But outside football, during his first year in Lincoln, Irving found college life depressing. The troubled freshman often found himself alone in his dormitory room while roommate Turner Gill appeared fairly content.

"It was tough at times. Turner had a car. I didn't. Turner could go whenever he wanted to go. I was stuck here. I didn't really know a whole lot of people, so that first year was kind of tough. It was kind of lonely. And I had never been away from home for any extended period of time at all."

He almost quit school during his first semester holiday vacation.

"I remember the first break I went home, it was Thanksgiving or Christmas, and I wasn't coming back. In fact, I stayed an extra week more than I was supposed to. I don't know if Tom [Osborne] knew about it or what, but I was missing classes because I wasn't coming back."

But he did return as family members provided the vital moral support.

"My mother was a trooper. There were times when her and my grandmother and my sisters would call and sing gospel songs over the phone. It was a time when I needed them. And my mother and my grandmother and my sisters were there for me.

"Going through college was a good time. And I wouldn't change it for the world. The Lord led me out to Nebraska. I didn't know I was being led by the Lord. I know it was all in His divine plan in my life."

Irving felt no frustrations with his on-field life in the heartland. Early on, Husker coaches opted to move him from the defensive secondary to the opposite side of the ball as a wingback. The decision bore monumental fruits. During his 1983 senior season, the consensus All-American wide receiver sped for a season total 1,267 all-purpose yards, including 40 receptions for 780. As one of the fastest Huskers in school history, he cruised to a 4.43 electronic clocking in the 40 yard dash. He hauled in passes with his 37-inch vertical leaping ability.

A member of the triplet's Scoring Explosion offense, he shared the backfield with Heisman Trophy winning I-back Mike Rozier and versatile three-time All-Big Eight quarterback Turner Gill. The 1983 Nebraska offense tallied an NCAA record 624 points during the regular season.

Irving found his collegiate career extremely satisfying and memorable, but there has been one negative play he has struggled to forget. It was a moment during the 1984 National Championship Orange Bowl loss to the University of Miami.

One minute and 12 seconds remained with the No. 1 Cornhuskers trailing the fifth-ranked Hurricanes 31-24. It was second and eight from the Miami 24-yard line. Quarterback Gill took the snap from center and the All-American receiver sprinted downfield. Turner fired to his favorite target in the end zone, but it dropped from Fryar's hands, incomplete.

"I just remember running down the middle of the field and the ball being thrown. I didn't let it get into my body and it bounced off my hip and hit the ground. We would have been one point down if I had caught the ball, but we scored two plays later anyway, so it really didn't make a difference.

"We lost that Orange Bowl [31-30] and people started saying that Irving Fryar dropped that pass on purpose and all that type of stuff. The memory that people always bring up to me when they see me is the fact that I dropped that ball. That's all that people ever seem to remember. So I can't forget about it because people won't let me forget about it."

Irving finished the night with a respectable 130 all-purpose yards, including five receptions for 65 yards, but for him the game's concluding moments were tormenting.

"I blamed myself for losing. It was all my fault as far as I was concerned. If you can take that load and place it on one person's shoulders—there I am, sitting with it on my shoulders."

And the pain has continued, he said.

"I never did cope with it, actually. Like I said, people still remind me of it. So, it still bothers me. It just motivated me to do better and not to let that situation happen again."

Life offered somewhat of a fresh start that spring as New England tabbed the New Jersey jet as the National Football League's overall No. 1 draft pick. But his prodigal lifestyle and inner turmoil followed him to his native east coast as well.

"I began to make some wrong decisions. I got involved in drugs. I started hanging around with the wrong people, going to the wrong places, doing the wrong things, getting a lot of bad press. Things were pretty bad for me. So I started to hibernate. I started not caring about people, not caring about myself, and hiding out in the house—insecurity, doubt. There was a time, even in there, when I tried to take my own life.

"There were a lot of things that kept me separated from Christ when I was in the world. There were drugs. There were women. And I just believe now that I have got to stand strong on the Word to keep me close to God, to keep me solid in the Word, and keep me solid in my faith."

In 1989, during Irving's fifth season with the New England Patriots, he realized he had made too many wrong decisions in life and that he wanted to permanently change. He had deliberately avoided God his whole life.

"I grew up in the church, so I knew right and wrong. I knew about Christ, and the Bible and all. At a certain point I found a church in Boston and I started going to that church. I was basically tired of being sick and tired. I didn't have any place to turn to. I had been convicted my whole life. Sometimes we pay attention to it, sometimes we don't. The Lord was tugging at my heart and I knew I had to do something about it. I would have probably wound up going down the drain.

"I finally got enough courage to say, 'God, I know I messed up.

You see all and You know all. God, if you can find it in Your heart to forgive me, have Your way with me. I'm so tired of being sick and tired. I'll do anything You want.' And before I could even finish praying that prayer, God saved me. He changed my life. He changed the way I talk. He fixed my home. I was looking for love in all the wrong places. I was looking for love in the streets. I was looking for love from women. I was looking for love from drugs, in the bars, in the bottle. The only and real true love is in Jesus Christ— that unconditional love that says, 'I will never leave you, nor forsake you.' (Joshua 1:5) I can't make it without Christ.

"All of the awards, all of the accolades, all of the nice things that people say to me, all of the TV, all of the money, all of that stuff doesn't amount to a hill of beans without knowing Jesus Christ."

As a new believer, Irving wanted to share his new found hope with others. He desired to enter the ministry. Even during his violent adolescence, he said he felt convicted to become a preacher one day.

"I had known I was supposed to be a preacher since I was 17 years old. My grandmother was always telling me that I was going to be a preacher, along with a few other people. When I rededicated myself, I felt my calling the same day."

Two years following his conversion, he was ordained in the Baptist and Pentecostal churches. He has not only shared his faith before congregations, but with teammates who have often been eager to listen.

"All the time, every day guys are constantly asking me questions about the Bible. They are asking me questions about their lives, concerning different situations, what they should do, how they should act or what they should say. It's something that goes on continually.

"I'm just like one of the guys. I don't walk around with my nose stuck up in the air or walk around saying, 'I'm a preacher' or walk around saying this or that. I act like a Christian, but I still laugh and have fun with the guys. They see that you can still be ordinary, so to speak, and be a Christian. There's a lot of people that think you have got to be unordinary to be a Christian."

The change within the wide receiver's life has been dramatic. Former Miami teammate, tight end Keith Jackson, recalled discovering Fryar's conversion shortly after he was traded from New England to the Dolphins in 1993.

"When I first met Irving, he was pretty wild," recounted Jackson. "He was pretty out there in the world. I think everybody could read about all the trouble he got into and the problems he was having. But I got a chance to really know Irving at Miami. And I said, 'This guy doesn't sound like the same guy that I read about. There's something different about him.' And I could see the difference in him. And I had the opportunity to ask him, and I said, 'Man, you're not the same guy I thought you were.' And he said, 'I'm a Christian now. And not only am I a Christian, I'm a minister. I'm a minister in the Word of God.'"

The pair often played on the field and stood on the sidelines together. They regularly pushed each other to take the high road during the volatile moments of a game.

"We kind of held each other accountable on the football field," stressed the 6-2, 258-pound receiver. "We can get a little upset during the game. People feel like when you're a Christian you're not supposed to get upset, but we kept each other calmed down. When we really wanted to retaliate on a guy who took a dirty hit on us and stuff, he would say, 'That's not the Christian thing to do.'"

Formerly a violent gang member, now a bold preacher, the native of Mount Holly, N.J. has found a new lease on life. Fryar, who once followed the turbulent ways of his peers, has sought to be like his Uncle Arnold and provide a positive influence for whomever he can minister.

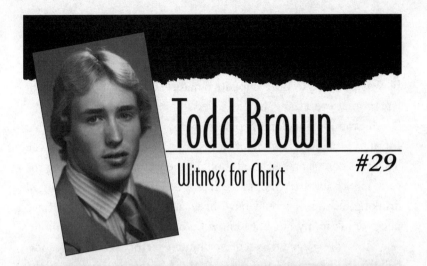

Todd Brown

Witness for Christ

#29

All-Big Eight Honorable Mention split end 1980, four-year letterman 1979-82

The struggle to find identity, purpose and to cope with peer pressure, have been components in the everyday life of an American teenager. And though they were not easy, for Todd Brown, those pre-adult years were a memorable period of positive growth and inspiration. During high school he felt a sense of mission and purpose to be part of a spiritual movement in the small central Nebraska town of Holdrege.

"God started a revival in our town," Todd reflected. "We had as many as 130 kids going to Fellowship of Christian Athletes out of a high school of 330. That's a pretty major impact.

"When I was a senior, every person on the varsity basketball team was a Christian, all 12 of us. If you played football, you really felt out of place if you weren't going to FCA.

"God was using positive peer pressure. We took our Bibles to school. We confronted kids who were partying. We took our faith seriously. We took it very seriously, but we were a very light-hearted, fun-loving group. We just tried to show the world that being a Christian is absolutely, positively the best life one could ever lead."

Brown described himself as driven, highly motivated, and having an addictive personality. Prior to becoming a Christian, he said he was enslaved to his competitive nature. Unless this all-state athlete won at everything, he had failed.

"I was looking for happiness in my life and tried to find it through athletics. The victories became shallower and shallower. That was confusing because I thought the victories would bring me to a higher level of happiness. If I ever would have ever started drinking alcohol, I would have been an alcoholic. In fact, I have never drank in my life, but I know I would have been an alcoholic.

"At a young age I decided the ultimate victory was to play football for the Huskers. I think there's a lot of football players at the University of Nebraska that think that. But when it's all over, they are in for serious letdowns because it's a short-lived thing. I just praise God that I was spared from that because I had things in perspective beforehand."

He said he found perspective following an FCA meeting some friends from his high school football team had invited him to attend. The speaker challenged him.

"Much to my surprise I realized I wasn't a Christian. I gave my life to Christ."

As a Christian, Brown said his passion turned into a deeply rooted faith, that offered him peace and purpose.

"God changed my life and my perspective. I have always been a pretty highly motivated person, but my motivation changed from one of self-glorification to one of wanting to glorify Christ. That gave me the meaning in life that I was looking for."

That decision impacted his family as well.

"Since then they have all become Christians. It's been really neat to see an organization like the Fellowship of Christian Athletes impact my whole family with the gospel. I don't think my parents have ever been to an FCA meeting, but I know they have been impacted by FCA in a tremendous way."

Inspired, the 16-year-old desired to share his newfound faith with anyone he came in contact with. He not only approached students, but fans and reporters as well.

"I looked at every success as an opportunity. I looked at every time anyone asked me about any accomplishments, that was my cue to tell them about Christ. Every reporter that asked me how long I had been working something, I shared Christ with them. I let them know where I was coming from. It wasn't printed in a lot of papers, but the person that was interviewing me heard the gospel."

He not only found success as a super-prep athlete on the football field, but in track as well. As a senior in 1978, he set the Nebraska high school all-class record in the triple jump at 50 feet, two-and-one-fourth-inches. Top track programs attempted to recruit him, he said. But the Nebraska native's heart was in football. He chose to walk-on to the Big Red.

"I was highly recruited as a track athlete, but the NCAA

wouldn't allow track scholars to play football. So I was not offered a football scholarship, but I was asked to walk-on."

Feeling the financial crunch of paying his own way during his first semester, Brown opted to focus his athletic energies where he could hold a scholarship.

"I made a decision that if I didn't receive a football scholarship, I would quit football and go out for track. But Coach Osborne found a scholarship for me that second semester. I don't know how he did it, but I'm thankful that he found one, because I knew that it was tough for him. By the same token, it was tough for me because I was going to pay for my own schooling. I was basically able to get school paid for a lot cheaper on a full-ride track scholarship."

The triple jumper competed for Nebraska's indoor track team during the spring of his freshman year. It would be his only collegiate track season as he chose to concentrate on football. Osborne's decision to elevate Brown from walk-on status proved to be an investment as the Holdrege native started three years at split end. The wide receiver played in several memorable games, including a 37-14 Big Eight Championship win over the Sooners at Norman in 1981, and in the controversial 1982 loss to the Nittany Lions at State College, Penn.

The lop-sided road victory over Barry Switzer's Sooners marked Osborne's first out-right Big Eight Championship.

"That was a pretty phenomenal game. Oklahoma was somebody I wanted to beat with all of my heart. And to just dominate them, it was wonderful. It had been a long dry spell for Nebraska. And then to come home to an airport that was just packed with people, that was definitely a highlight. I really appreciated the fans at that point. I had broken my nose in the game and could have really cared less when we got home."

No. 2 Nebraska's loss at Beaver Stadium Sept. 25, 1982 has been remembered by two key controversial plays during eventual National Champion Penn State's winning drive.

After trailing the entire game, Nebraska quarterback Turner Gill capped an 80-yard 13-play drive with a 1-yard touchdown plunge for the go-ahead score late in the fourth quarter. But it was not over yet.

On the next series, with the ball on their own 35 and 1:18 left to play, eighth-ranked Penn State trailed 24-21. The Nittany Lion offense would would cover the distance in 10 plays, as quarterback Todd Blackledge completed five of eight passes for 60 yards. On second and four at the Nebraska 17 with short seconds remaining, the Penn State quarterback hit receiver Mike McCloskey for 15 yards. Taped replays indicate the ball was caught out of bounds. The following play, Blackledge's low 2-yard pass to receiver Kirk Bowman was ruled complete in the end zone with four seconds on the clock. Penn State blew the PAT kick, thus the final, the Nittany Lions 27, Cornhuskers 24. Replays show the ball may have been trapped on that game winning touchdown pass.

"It was a complete drop," Brown stated. "It wasn't even close enough to be a trap. The play that was worse than that was the play where the ball was caught out of bounds. I could see it. That was really frustrating, too, because I couldn't play because the defense was on the field. We just had to stand and watch.

"But by the same token, I'm just happy to have been part of a game like that. It was just the opportunity to be there and experience that. Since the beginning of the season everybody knew that was for the national championship, and it was. If we'd win that game, we'd win it all. Everybody in the whole wide world knew that we got robbed. But we couldn't whine about it.

"I just count it as a blessing to have been a part of not only that, but under the teaching and character of coach Osborne. Those are the things that I remember.

"Coach Osborne just came in the locker room and said, 'Guys, when you're in a big game like this, you just have to play so much better than them that nothing can take that victory away from you.'

"And we just said, 'Hey, we didn't win.'

"I appreciated that so much from a godly man. Coach Osborne influences so many people and I don't think he'll ever know how much he has influenced me and many, many other people, too.

"But that really set the tone. We just said, 'Next time we just really better beat them by a whole bunch.'"

A week later, a road game with 20th-ranked Auburn would test No. 8 Nebraska's resiliency.

"That would have been a game we could have easily let down. I remember running out onto the field and the fans threw corn cobs at us," Todd laughed.

Brown also recalled watching a then little-known freshman Auburn tailback.

"I was standing on the sideline watching a young man who nobody knew about. But he was faster than anybody that I'd ever seen–Bo Jackson!"

Deadlocked at seven through most of the first half, it looked to be a battle the rest of the way until Husker quarterback Gill completed a 58-yard touchdown pass to Brown with 3:32 left before intermission.

"It was third and 18 and they [Auburn] should've been in a prevent defense. But we caught them and scored a touchdown, which really broke their back.

"Their corner had been pressuring me a lot when I was running short routes, trying to pick the ball off. So I ran a hook-and-go. I would run like I was going to run a hook-play and when the guy comes up, I'd just go on by him. He bit really hard on the hook move and I got behind him and [quarterback] Turner [Gill] put the ball on the money. We went in at the half with seven more points than we should have. That was a pivotal play in the game. They got discouraged and we ended up really putting it to them [winning 41-7]. That was a pretty crucial game in our season."

The Huskers wrapped up the remainder of the year undefeated, with an overall 12-1 record and a second conference crown. Following a 21-20 Orange Bowl win over 13th ranked Louisiana State, the Huskers trailed only Penn State and Southern Methodist in the final polls.

Brown wrapped up his senior season with 23 catches for 398 yards and four touchdowns. The senior from Holdrege was drafted in the sixth-round by the Detroit Lions, but he opted to play Canadian ball.

As a Montreal Concorde, he said he was listed among the league's top receivers. Nevertheless he found himself unemployed in his third season in 1985 as the team fell upon financially hard times. General management attempted to salvage the organization by cutting players and American athletes tended to be the first to go. The former Husker received the bad news in the coach's office. And though football had been a passion for him, Todd was not shaken.

"My wife Michele was pregnant with our twins and I was called into the coach's office.

"He said, 'Todd, I've got some bad news. We're going to have to release you.'

"It was funny. Just the day before my name was in the paper because I was named to an all-pro team. They were having financial troubles. And by the world's standards that was probably a pretty dark day.

"But God was glorified in that I just told the coach, 'Nothing that happens to me happens without passing through my Father's hands. You may think you control what happens today, but this is God. And don't worry about it.'

"He was very choked up and gave me a hug and just kind of shook his head. It was just a real opportunity to minister. I knew that my getting cut was part of God's plan. And if God didn't want me to play for that team, I wasn't going to play for them. And that's exactly what happened. God was ready for me to move on.

"And what would be a terrible time, from the world's standpoint–I mean, I got fired from my job," Todd chuckled, "was a tremendous victory in Christ. I count that as one of my most treasured times, in terms of being able to walk the walk and mean it."

Other players were eventually let go from the club as the Montreal Concordes ended up folding, Brown said.

But during his playing time in Montreal, Todd was reunited with a former Husker teammate, quarterback Turner Gill.

Gill, perhaps, was the prototype option signal caller. His skills were tailored to the Canadian style offense. The Concorde coaching staff asked Brown's opinion of Gill during the scouting process.

"'I think Turner is the best quarterback in the country,' he told staff members. "And I still think that. If I could pick one quarterback in the whole world to have on my team, I'd pick Turner Gill, without any questions. We just didn't lose ball games when he was pulling the trigger. They asked me about him and I said that he was the best quarterback that I had ever seen. He was having a phenomenal season in '83 as a quarterback. They basically stole him away from the NFL draft. I was really happy."

At the university, Brown and Gill were casual in their friendship, but the pair became close at the professional level.

"Turner and I became closer friends. I didn't know him very well in college, but in Canada we spent some time together. Whenever we would go on road trips, Turner would come down to my room and we'd talk. I'd always share the gospel with him."

Gill asked several questions and grew eager to discuss spiritual matters. The former Husker quarterback eventually accepted Christ and now boldly shares his faith with others as well–because one individual desired to pass that good news on to him.

Brown spent two more years in the Canadian Football League.

From 1987, through part of the '88 season, he played for the Saskatchewan Roughriders. He finished his professional career in 1988 with the Winnipeg Blue Bombers. Since his football career Todd Brown has served as vice president and part-owner, with his father, of Jim Brown Construction in Holdrege, Neb. He is also the owner and president of Church Design Architects.

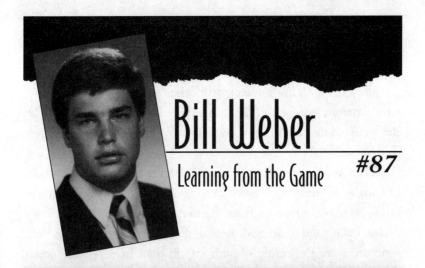

Bill Weber

Learning from the Game

#87

*All-Big Eight defensive end 1984,
Academic All-Big Eight 1982-84,
four-year letterman 1981-84*

Nebraska's Blackshirts had given up 300 passing yards and four touchdowns en route to a devastating 31-30 national championship loss to Miami in the Jan. 2, 1984 Orange Bowl. Though painful, the days following that fateful night were a period of learning for former NU defensive end Bill Weber. A three-year starter and academic all-conference honoree in 1982-84, the Lincoln, Neb. native has placed a high value on the maturity process.

"I like to think about what you learn from experiences–what you can take from it and apply to your life and how valuable it can be," the 1984 All-Big Eight defensive end explained. "It's funny how you don't realize those things when you're going through them. As an 18-to-22 year-old you're not mature enough to comprehend why things happen the way they do. It's only after that you are mature and have a little time to reflect. It's then that you learn what you can take and apply in other areas of your life."

Weber was typically quiet and independent. The 1980 state prep athlete of the year from Lincoln Southeast spent much college free time studying the Bible, he said.

"During the playing season I needed to get away from the university for a day. I spent a lot of time reading on Sunday after church. I really didn't interact with other guys a lot, I don't know why. There was never a dull moment reading. I was just struck by the tremendous truth that comes through in any part of the New Testament."

The Christian faith has fathomed deep in Bill Weber's heritage. Originally of Germanic descent, he explained how his grandfathers immigrated to America from Russia in the early 1900s. They brought the values and traditions of their homeland. God and the scripture were the center of authority in their lives. Those forefathers had grown within close-knit families and communities. Churches lined several square blocks in their homeland. A place of worship could often be found within walking distance.

Bill said he accepted Christ as a teenager. He has since sought to grow in that personal relationship with his Savior. The former student athlete has maintained a private disciplined lifestyle. He has seen solitude as an opportunity for reflection. He has grown to appreciate the process and lessons of life. Many of those lessons trace their roots from the athletic field.

"There's no comparison to what I can take from athletics versus what I can take from my academic experience. The challenges I was forced to face in athletics helped me grow personally so much more than the challenges I faced in the class room.

"We as a society need to support extracurricular activities, whether it be athletics or something else. Because that's where people really learn and grow. I don't think you learn discipline or how to deal with adversity by studying a textbook. You learn those things by applying your abilities in some kind of real-world setting. And I think we need to support those kind of activities in some way."

Weber competed in eleven championship games during his

youth and collegiate career. The Cornhuskers' six-foot-two-inch, 210-pound defensive lineman played opposite the Miami Hurricanes during the fateful '84 National Championship Orange Bowl. He contributed in 10 Nebraska Class A State Championship games during his football, basketball, and baseball tenure at Lincoln Southeast High School. And from those wins and losses he continually found new ways he needed to develop. And the heart-breaking 31-30 Orange Bowl loss to Miami provided an invaluable opportunity for that.

"It was a very frustrating game for me, because you just sensed that the opportunity was slipping away. We wanted to win so badly that I think it affected our ability to play. It's been difficult to live with knowing that you had an opportunity to win the national championship, being so close and lose it. But life goes on. Whether you win it or lose it, you're not any better of a person, you are not any more or less successful. You still have to go to work and perform.

"Looking back, I realize that our pursuit of the national championship was taken too seriously by some fans. Football is still a game. Things happen that you can't control. Some games you lose and some games you win and you're not a better or worse person because of it. That took me some time to realize and understand that.

"Obviously, Tom Osborne is a very successful coach whether he won the national championship or not. But a lot of people would say he wasn't truly a great coach until he won those championships. Well, I mean, that's just ludicrous."

From that game, Bill learned to play more loose and confident. As a senior, it motivated him to better respect his opponents. The pain from the loss built a fire under the defensive unit. The 1984 squad would lead the nation in fewest average yards allowed (203.3) and average points given up each game (9.5) during the season. The Huskers' rushing defense finished fourth nationally. But the biggest improvement came in their pass defense as they ranked fifth. The 1984 Huskers gave up only 124.5 yards per game through the air after allowing an average 218.9 in '83.

"We all stepped it up a notch. We put in some new schemes that started to work. We brought in some depth. We played with more confidence because when you've been to the top of the mountain and pushed down, it's easier to fight that same battle."

The 1984 Huskers finished the season with a 10-2 record, including a 28-10 Sugar Bowl victory over Louisiana State. In the polls, they closed out the year ranked third in UPI and fourth in AP.

Amidst the rough defensive front line, Weber said one of his biggest challenges was avoiding trash talking. He especially wanted to honor God in the heat of battle.

"In athletics there's a lot of ungodly activity going on. There's a lot of trash talking and egotistical people in athletics. There are a lot of negative things that, quite frankly, make it difficult at times to compete and maintain a Christian attitude. I made a vow that I would keep my mouth shut on the football field. I can't say I was successful all the time, but I really wanted to respect the people I played against and not belittle them in any way."

As Weber reflected on his career, he sited the coaching philosophies of his former high school coach and NU's present assistant head coach/running backs coach, Frank Solich, as instrumental to developing his philosophies on the game. Solich, a former Husker All-Big Eight player in his day, played with a positive mental attitude. Weighing less than 160 pounds, the Ohio native played fullback and was a co-captain on Nebraska's 1965 squad.

"Coach Solich epitomizes the competitive spirit. It's in his nature, maybe because he's a little undersized. He had to work that much harder and be that much more aggressive when he was a player. He really had a big influence on me in that regard. You can talk about talent and ability, but it really comes from the heart whether you win. And coach Solich really drove that home for me and for all the players that play for him."

In 1989-90 Weber returned to UNL as a graduate assistant football coach after quitting his position as a federal bank examiner. In 1990 he played dual roles as the head freshman coach. A family man, he has since served as the Vice President of Corporate Banking at Norwest Nebraska in Lincoln. There he has continued to apply the principles of learning.

The Latter 1980s
Cornhuskers for Christ

Former fullback Ken Kaelin attributed the examples of former Nebraska football players like Todd Brown and George Andrews as instrumental in his conversion as a 16-year old. Brown and Andrews together shared their faith at a Fellowship of Christian Athletes event at Midlands College in March 1980, he said.

Thus, as an upperclassmen in the mid-80s, Kaelin and offensive guard Stan Parker pooled together a corps of teammates who shared a common desire to spread the gospel. They called themselves Cornhuskers for Christ. For one week during January 1986 and '87 following the bowl games, about 10 players piled into a van and traveled to different central Nebraska churches, civic meetings, and schools to speak. They used the platform of Nebraska football to share Christ with many youth within the state.

Former offensive guard Mike Hoefler described his memories on the road sharing his faith.

"We had about 10 Christian football players who hopped in a van and we went to high schools and had altar calls. And when you pray to lead somebody to Christ, that is just awesome."

Brad Johnson, a former offensive lineman, recalled the response after speaking at a public high school.

"We all shared our faith and I was just shocked at the response. I literally had 15 or 20 kids surrounding me who wanted to trust Christ. And I remember I was somewhat skeptical. I was asking them, 'Now, are you sure you know what this means? This means you will become a Christian and will go to heaven.' And everyone of them said,'Yes. Absolutely. I know what this means.'

"And I thought maybe it was the notoriety of the football [program]. But it seemed that the message was really the thing and that the Lord was really working in their hearts. So that was exciting."

Seeds to reach out to others were planted inside former fullback Sam Schmidt following his graduation. With his wife Kristen, the couple has served as house parents to junior high age boys at Boys Town in Omaha, Neb.

When asked what he found most fulfilling in his opportunity to minister to young people, Sam replied, "I don't necessarily find the things that we do, fulfilling, in and of themselves. I look more at being obedient and serving the Lord. That's what's fulfilling about this—doing whatever it is that the Lord would have us do. I wouldn't want to find fulfillment in the act itself, but in the obedience and service to the Lord, for whatever he would have us do."

For the members of "Cornhuskers for Christ," those days of sharing their faith touched far more people than their audiences. It touched the lives of each athlete, as well.

Stan Parker

An Eternal Perspective

#74

The late November scenario of that intense rivalry was all too familiar. Over 76,000 screaming fans filled the stands in Lincoln's Memorial Stadium. Both teams were ranked inside the top-five and the Big Eight Championship and trip to the Orange Bowl were on the line. Barry Switzer stood on opposite sidelines from Tom Osborne. It was them versus us. The sight seemed unlikely, even as it happened–yet on Nov. 22, 1986, about a dozen Nebraska and Oklahoma players huddled at mid-field before kickoff to pray. Some kneeled, others stood hand-in-hand.

That mental image from his senior season has engraved itself within Stan Parker's memories. It has represented the former Cornhusker offensive guard and captain's life perspective–viewing his existence in light of eternity. With his football career's biggest game at hand, he gathered with rival players to worship God.

Some years earlier as a redshirt freshman, he sat quietly in his dorm room after undergoing physical therapy for a knee injury suffered in a post-high school Shrine bowl game. The underclassman contemplated the successes he had found over the past two years of his life, yet the former Prep All-American of Bellevue East felt an overwhelming emptiness inside.

Originally recruited as a tight end, the 6-foot-5, 245-pound lineman had turned away offers from various major universities. He recorded the nation's second longest discus throw, at 195 feet, seven inches after winning the Class A heavy weight wrestling title as a prep senior.

"As a non-Christian, I came to the place where I realized that the world had nothing for me. I knew there weren't any other options. I remember thinking, 'You mean that's all there is in this world?'

"My biggest lows were not circumstantial. Mine were recognitions of the emptiness of success. I dated the cheerleaders. I had a new car, I had a scholarship, I had decent grades. There weren't any circumstantial things that were low for me. But in the midst of experiencing those successes, I was empty. And I was very acutely aware of that emptiness."

The tall lineman explained realizing the brevity of life's accomplishments and it's cycle of emotional extremes.

"I recall asking myself, 'Is that what life's about, an occasional high point, but then just kind of existing?' Then he thought to himself, 'Maybe it's God that I'm missing.'"

Parker looked at the floor, alone with his thoughts. He even wondered if he even believed in God. The young man pushed his questions aside.

Over one year passed and he moved into an apartment and was befriended by a Christian neighbor.

"Through that relationship I saw the reality of Christ in his life. He had a lot of things that I admired. He had a peace, purpose, joy and meaning. And those were all the things that I was lacking. So I was drawn to him.

"Yet, as I look back at that time, if the world would have looked back at he and I, they would have said that I had it all. But at that time, I realized he had it all."

Looking back, the former lineman said God used the neighbor's example to prepare him for hearing the gospel. Parker was more than willing to hear and talk about it for several hours. His questions about life did not end with that discussion. He wrestled with them intensely for the next two weeks as he studied from a Bible he borrowed. And through his study, Parker said that he realized the extent of his sin and the need for Jesus Christ to pay for sin's penalty on the cross.

The young athlete's questions turned from, "How can a loving God send anyone to hell?" to, "How can a just God let me into heaven?"

Parker said he recognized his inability to meet God's standard of holiness. Jesus Christ had already met God's requirement as the only perfect sacrifice for the history of the human race. And only through repentance and faith in Christ, Stan explained, could he have that eternal relationship with God and purpose that he was missing. At that point, Stan asked Christ to be his Lord and Savior.

"And then a process began and God began to make me into what He wanted me to be," Stan smiled. "He began to deal with my thought life, my language, my priorities, and with my motivations for doing things. He just began to deal with every area of my life—my relationship with my family, and my relationship with friends."

The student-athlete sought to grow in his faith by studying the Bible. An older college student offered various study guides to help him learn. Parker also borrowed sermon tapes to aid, as well. That fall, the offensive lineman's teammates noticed a definite change.

"There was no more cursing and no more parties. I was talking about Jesus," Stan chuckled. "I didn't hear anything real negative from it. I had a little of that zeal without knowledge that a lot of new believers have—where I pushed it a little too hard on people. But, I did that mainly with my family. Among friends and people that I knew, I think they were pretty open to it."

As the college student grew in his new faith, he deeply contemplated quitting football to serve God in some unknown way. In hindsight, Parker said his youthful zeal was sincere, but he was lacking in refined wisdom.

"I was a new Christian who had not been raised religious. I didn't know what ministry was, all I knew was I wanted to give my life to eternal things. I didn't know what that meant. But I wanted to get to know God better. 'People are dying and going to hell and I'm playing a game?' That's how I felt. I wrestled with that. But I just felt like God said, 'Be patient and be faithful where you're at. Use every opportunity you get to share with others and learn and grow. I mean, what would a new Christian have done in ministry full time? Because, looking back, I feel God was saying, 'You're in a good enough place for me to prepare you. So just stay there."

Parker plunged into his spiritual life with both feet. He explained that his greatest desire has been to live each day with an eternal perspective.

"I see a lot of Christians that, in my mind, are not convinced that the world doesn't have anything for them. So they still struggle. I'm not necessarily talking about a sin issue. I'm talking about abandoning it all. 'This world has nothing for me. I'm selling out to God. He's all that I want. He's all that I need.'

"One of my favorite Psalms [Psalm 73:25], says, 'Whom have I in heaven but you? And earth has nothing I desire besides you.' (NIV)

"And as a non-Christian I came to the place where I was convinced that the world had nothing for me. Now, as a non-Christian, that scared me to death. I'm going, that's all there is in this world? So, when I came to Christ, I realized 'There's nothing to hold back on.' I wanted more of this."

As he endeavored with his collegiate gridiron career, he actively sought opportunities to share his faith. He regularly fulfilled autograph requests with that underlying purpose in mind.

"I'd sign my autograph and write 'G-T-G-T-G' below it and wait for the kids to come back and ask what it meant. And they often did return and were open to hearing what it meant, which is, Give The Glory To God."

During his upperclassmen years, his close friend and teammate, fullback Ken Kaelin of Westerville, Neb., organized annual week-long excursions to central Nebraska immediately following the winter's bowl game. Parker, Kaelin and about eight other teammates would pile into a van to speak at various small towns. The corps, who dubbed themselves "Cornhuskers for Christ" shared their faith in churches, various club meetings, and even public schools. They spoke anywhere the opportunity was freely given.

Stan recalled a public high school student who heard the message at such a meeting.

"There was a foreign exchange student who was going back to Australia two days later. And she ended up trusting Christ before she went home. I stayed in contact with her for awhile. I remember praying some specific things for her that God would provide good Christian fellowship. And she wrote me later and her words were almost exactly what I had prayed."

On the field, Stan started at right guard during his last two seasons. A moment in time in Ames, Iowa, not likely remembered by anyone else, has been among his favorite game reminiscences. It was during a 35-14 beating of Iowa State on Nov. 8, 1986. During the matchup, the lineman turned to Kaelin and told him to follow his block if a trap-play was called.

"We got close to the goal line at one point and the play was called for Ken," Stan recalled. "He did what I told him to do and just rode my back right into the end zone.

"I hit the linebacker and turned over. Ken landed right on top of me. We just looked at each other face-to-face in the end zone, got up and praised God."

Two weeks later was the shootout of the year when the defending National Champion Oklahoma Sooners came to Lincoln. The Friday evening prior to game day was the regular team movie night. And by coincidence, the rival squads simultaneously attended the same theater and movie. No unfriendly incident occurred. Parker sought out running back Spencer Tilman, who he knew was a fellow Christian. The pair left the theater and hung out at a yogurt parlor. There they agreed to gather other interested teammates to meet at mid-field before kickoff and pray. Parker said he had never heard of players meeting for such a thing before on the gridiron.

"I don't know if this had been done before. Now, it happens all the time. Then, even after a game, you never saw that. It was sort of a new concept.

"It was a great feeling in the sense of contrast. That was very evident. I mean, this wasn't a love relationship between Nebraska and Oklahoma. And to be able to come together in the spirit of Christ and connect was such a contrast and at the same time to make a statement to those watching that we stood for something different."

The No. 5 Huskers suited up in all red uniforms in anticipation of the nationally televised matchup with their third-ranked opponent. Nebraska scored first midway through the opening quarter and took a 17-7 lead into the fourth period. But after trailing most of the afternoon, Oklahoma scored 10 points in the game's closing 90 seconds to win 20-17 and secure a berth in the Orange Bowl. Sooner kicker Tim Lasher's field goal with 10:39 left and a 17-yard Jamelle Holieway to Keith Jackson pass with 1:22 remaining would tie the game. Oklahoma then held the Husker offense on four straight downs. With 50 seconds on the clock and Sooner Magic alive and kicking, Oklahoma marched 51 yards to the Nebraska 14-yard line. Six seconds remained as Tim Lasher then booted a 31-yard field goal for the 20-17 win.

"I was in shock," Stan said recalling Lasher's kick through the uprights. "Before the last two minutes I was emotionally high. To see that taken away in two minutes, I got emotional whiplash. I was just kind of numb."

That spring the defending Super Bowl Champion New York Giants drafted Parker in the ninth round of the NFL draft. He reported to training camp in the summer. With a business degree in hand, the offensive guard didn't know to do with his life. He had checked various possibilities in the business field and he felt no strong passion toward playing in the NFL. His desire lay within ministry.

"Coming out of college, I felt God was speaking to me to just do the next thing. I felt like God was saying, 'I'll lead you.' I checked doors within the business realm and nothing seemed like it was a natural thing. So I said, 'OK, this [trying out for the NFL] is the next thing.' But I never felt like I wanted to make the team. I didn't feel this was the next thing I was going to give my life to—which is a major reason why I didn't make the team. Because you have to say, 'I want this' to even have a shot. Because I was just like, 'I'll see what happens. I'll try it.'"

Yet, opportunities to minister to others were continually before him. As prospective players piled into camp, he focused on the task at hand. He would practice hard, pray, and see what happens. And while settling down in his room, his first ministry opportunity presented himself.

"Right off the bat I felt God had placed me there. When I checked in, one of the other rookies showed up with just a loud foul mouth. And I was thinking, 'Boy, I hope he's not my roommate.'" Stan shared with a smile in his voice.

And as it would turn out, they were assigned to the same quarters.

"I was just thinking, 'Oh, my goodness.'" Stan laughed in recollection. "The first day, I was sitting in our room listening to some music, and he says,

"'Is that Christian music?'

And I go, 'Yeah. What do you know about that?'

"'Are you born again?'"

"'Yeah. What do you know about *that?*'

"'My brother's born again.'

The roommate responded with a low, somewhat irritated, and yet amused voice.

"And, that was the door. We talked about God often."

The linebacker even asked Parker to read the Bible to him. Stan had something within that the new roommate appeared to long for. The former Nebraska lineman was different from most of the other players at training camp. But then, one morning Parker got the typically dreaded knock on his door at 5:30 a.m.

"'Coach Bill Parcells wants to see you and bring your play-book,'" Parker recalled the voice from his doorway.

He was being cut. Stan looked over at his roommate who lay in bed crying.

"What am I going to do without you?" the linebacker sobbed.

Parker was touched.

"He was no wimp," Stan described the saddened roommate. "This is a guy, where Parcells made him mad one day in practice. And he was going against the No. 1 offense and an all-pro guard. And it was live on the line. So, they ran this pitch play and he hit this all-pro guard so hard. I've never seen anyone get hit so hard. He snapped his head back and knocked him backwards into the ball carrier. And knocked the ball carrier down. And then he stood over him, just shaking and breathing heavily," Stan mused.

"This was the guy who had tears streaming down his face and said, 'What am I going to do without you?' He didn't trust Christ that week. So I don't know where he's at today. But we shared some meaningful stuff. And I know why God had me there for that period of time."

Parker did not leave training camp without a job, though. During that stay, he made contact with Wendell Conover, the Nebraska director of the Fellowship of Christians Athletes, about an FCA representative position in Omaha which had opened up. The job was Stan's if he wanted it.

"I had been praying and wrestling through what God wanted me to do. I got convinced that it was in FCA. The next day I heard there was a spot open. So I called Wendell and set things in motion before I was released. I knew it was what I wanted to do. I knew that it was what God wanted me to do. So it wasn't a sad thing for me when I was cut."

For the next six years, Stan served within FCA. During that period he joined Keith Davey of Campus Crusade in presenting the gospel to new freshmen Nebraska football players. The two conducted surveys with many of the freshmen football players. Following the questionnaire, Parker and Davey would often follow-up with a discussion about Christianity.

And through his many experiences in FCA, Stan desired for deeper ministry involvement. He wanted to serve somewhere as a pastor.

"I got to a place where the vision God had given for me in ministry was bigger than what FCA could do. Fellowship of Christian Athletes is a very effective evangelistic tool, but that's all it is. I wanted to see someone come to Christ, be discipled, be grafted into the body, and the whole deal."

And since 1994, the former lineman has served as an assistant pastor at First Evangelical Free Church in Lincoln. And however he continues in ministry, his desire will remain to work for what bears eternal significance.

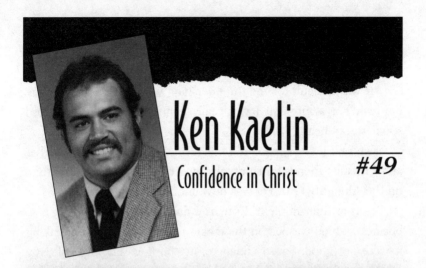

Ken Kaelin

Confidence in Christ

#49

**Three-year letterman
at fullback 1984-86**

He longed for the tranquility and splendor of the Colorado blue sky and Pikes Peak that loomed outside the hospital window.

Ken Kaelin was a durable fullback product of Ansley's eight-man football program in the central Nebraska sandhills. Typically confident and distinguished by a thick black mustache outlining his hearty likeable smile, he stood alone in anger and brokenness.

He and his wife Jamie recently moved away from their loved ones in the heartland and invested their entire savings into a partial business ownership in Colorado Springs. And now, the two people most intimate to him, Jamie and their unborn child, were suffering.

The doctor just informed him that Jamie and the baby's lives were at risk due to pregnancy complications. Jamie, who was six months pregnant, would require an emergency cesarean section for the baby to survive. In tears and silence he continued to stare through the pane.

"There was so much anger welled up in me," Ken recounted. "For the first time in my life I was angry at God. My wife was basically all I had and the doctor had told me that her life was in danger. This little baby we were looking so forward to, her chances were slim to none.

"It was difficult for me to understand what God's plan for my life was. For a moment I was really angry. Then I felt the Lord spoke to my heart."

Ken said he had relied too much on the support of his mother and Christian friends for spiritual strength and wisdom, rather than on the Almighty One. He was now admittedly, vulnerable.

"And at that moment, I saw my finances–I had started a new business, which was just in the making and our chances of making it were not good. So, my finances, my business life, my wife, my mom, my friends, everything was gone–at that moment. At that moment I saw everything as being gone."

Those things were not gone, however. For the time being, they were just out of reach.

"That's when I realized that all those things are awesome in my life. And I'm blessed with Christian friends and a Christian wife, and children, and my mom. All these people–I'm probably blessed more than any Christian I know with those things. But from that day on, my faith has been more personal to me than it ever was before. And my personal faith with Jesus Christ is more intense."

Jamie and the tiny newborn survived the painful birth. Kensy Lynn Kaelin was born three months premature on May 4, 1990 with cerebral palsy. She weighed two pounds and one ounce.

"Her body was smaller than my hand," Ken described.

The following days were difficult for the Kaelins as their tiny infant's chances of survival were unknown. Within days Kensy was able to breathe on her own and was eventually released from the hospital after two months.

"She started making progress. She was supposed to be in the hospital for three months. And Jamie recovered in five days and was able to see Kensy.

"That was an intense period of time," Ken sighed.

The Kaelins eventually left Colorado Springs to live in Omaha. There in southern Nebraska, Jamie gave birth to a healthy son named Kameron James. Yes, the road has been challenging since their daughter's birth complications, but Ken noted the remarkable strides in her life since.

"She's getting to the point now where all that's wrong with her are in the lower extremities. And as far as we're concerned, God healed her. She walks with very small braces to help her ankles and feet.

"In March 1995 she had massive surgeries done–spinal surgery, then hamstring surgery, and then surgery in her calf. She has done very well since the surgeries. And as far as I'm concerned, I've asked the Lord to heal her and He has.

"That surgery was the last episode and I probably cried harder than on the day she was born. Because we didn't decide that thing [her premature birth and complications]. That happened. And this thing [the surgeries], it took us two years to make the decision."

Prior to her surgery, his church congregation prayed for her healing during the operation.

"The way that I look at God, I'm not into demanding God into doing anything. I'm very respectful of my God. But He said to make our requests known, and so I did."

God would provide that needed grace, he believed–grace for both Kensy, himself and his wife.

He said she claimed the promise in 2 Corinthians 12:9-10, "But He [God] said to me, 'My grace is sufficient for you, for my power is made perfect in weakness. Therefore I will boast all the more gladly about my weaknesses, so that Christ's power may rest on me. That is why, for Christ's sake, I delight in weaknesses, in insults, in hardships, in persecutions, in difficulties. For when I am weak, then I am strong.'"

Typically an independent, self-reliant man who despised weakness, Ken felt God used his struggles to develop a greater trust in the Savior–rather than on his own insufficient energies.

"Never in my life had I referred to myself with this verse," Ken noted. "I had read it many times, but it never seemed to apply to me. Because the true strength would not be in me, but in the Lord. That was the ultimate thing I was able to find. That verse would sum it up completely."

On a similar theme, Ken recalled his final home game at Nebraska when he says God provided the needed strength and confidence to perform. That proudest and most memorable time was, ironically, a heart-breaking loss to the University of Oklahoma on November 22, 1986.

The stocky 5-foot-10-inch fullback played head-to-head with one of the highest regarded collegiate linebackers of all time, Brian Bosworth. The towering orange-haired, trash talking "Boz" symbolized the Sooners' swaggering style. Nebraska and Oklahoma were ranked fifth and third, respectively, by the Associated Press. The Sooners were the 1985 defending national champions. And Bosworth was on his way to winning his second Butkus Award as the nation's best linebacker.

"They were touting him as the greatest linebacker to ever play– I mean, Dick Butkus and everybody. They thought Brian Bosworth was taking it to a new level. And so, that's all we heard about all year. Most of the offensive lineman had this cover of this *Sports Illustrated* in their locker, waiting for the opportunity to play against this guy.

"And the night before [the game], running back Keith Jones and I were in our room watching the news. Brian Bosworth was staring at the camera and he says, 'Last year they had [fullback Tom] Rathman and [I-back Doug] Dubose. This year they don't have nothing.'

"I looked at Keith and he was talking straight to us. I mean, there was nobody he was talking to other than to tell us that Keith Jones and I were nothing. And compared to Tom Rathman [who went on to start for the Super Bowl Champion San Francisco 49ers] I was a step down. But Keith Jones was a phenomenal running back.

"As an overall football player, I couldn't compete with a Tom Rathman. But Tom Rathman taught me a lot of stuff he knew. [And] as a blocker, I knew I could block anybody I had faced so far. And in our offense, the fullback was hitting the linebacker 90 percent of the plays. So in Bosworth's mind, he thought it was going to be a cakewalk.

"I knew I had a great coach in Tom Osborne and a great [running backs] coach in Frank Solich. I felt they had prepared me to be the best football player that I could be. But I was also emotionally ready to play. I had no fear of this guy, whatsoever. I had doubts whether this guy would knock me cold. I didn't know if on national TV if this guy was what everybody said he was. I knew without a doubt that I would not crumble in front of him, because with Jesus Christ in my heart, I feared nothing. I was sure that I could hold my own against him if I depended on the Lord for my strength.

"And so, one of the articles in *Sports Illustrated* said, when he gets running backs down, one of the things that he would do is spit in their face. And I had all these visions of this happening.

"And one play, wingback Dana Brinson was supposed to crack back on Brian Bosworth. He was the only guy that touches the linebacker on a trap play that I would run. Well, I came off tackle and Dana Brinson kind of accidently slipped or something and never even touched him. And my fingers touched the ball and Brian Bosworth absolutely flattened me. I mean I was just on my back. His face mask hit under my chin and put me on my back. Then his face mask was right on my face mask. And he was looking right at me in my eyes and I was thinking, 'If this guy spits on me, Lord, only You know what I'll do.'

"And he never said a word. He never spit. He didn't do nothing. He just looked at me and got right up."

The blocking back noted that he and Bosworth exchanged hard hits throughout the game.

Nebraska drew first blood on a Keith Jones off tackle 2-yard touchdown run midway through the first quarter. It was the first rushing score recorded on the Oklahoma defense that season, Kaelin said.

"We continued to hit each other many times throughout the game. And not once did he do anything or say anything to me or any other players, that I remember. But on the sideline, he'd be yelling at the camera holding up oranges, in his orange hair and stuff. Saying stuff to the press. We found out that this was a show and that was what it was all about. He wasn't as bad as what we all thought."

And despite Bosworth and the fleet Sooner wishbone offense, the Cornhuskers held the momentum and the lead, 17-7, going into the fourth quarter. But in typical "Sooner Magic" fashion, coach Barry Switzer's squad would rally late in the final period.

Tim Lasher capped a 13-play Sooner drive with a 22-yard field goal with 10:39 remaining to close the margin to seven.

But it was All-American tight end Keith Jackson who grabbed two key receptions in the closing minutes. With 1:22 remaining, he scored on a 17-yard touchdown pass from Jamelle Holieway to tie the game at 17. And with nine seconds on the clock, he snagged a dramatic 41-yard pass on third down to set up a 31-yard game-winning field goal by Lasher. The final score, Oklahoma 20, Nebraska 17.

Players, coaches and media members jammed the crowded field following the game. Kaelin sought out Sooner running back Spencer Tilman. The pair, along with other teammates, had prayed together before the contest at mid-field.

"After the game was over, which was an incredible game, I saw Spencer Tilman and gave him a big hug. I told him it was the greatest game I had ever had a chance to play in. And I was turning around to walk back to the locker room and guess who was standing there–Brian Bosworth. And he's staring right at me. His orange hair was sweaty and running down into his face. He came walking straight up to me. And he's probably 6-foot-3 and I'm about 5-foot-10. And he walks up to me shaking his head. He's just standing there staring at me in disbelief. And he came up to me and hugged me. I just don't think that he really knew what to say. He said, 'Way to hit out there.'

"I'm sure he was shocked by how hard I hit him during the game. I looked at him and said, 'Hey, you too.'

"As I walked away, I didn't have anything else to say. And the truth of it all was, it was Jesus Christ who helped me to play at a much higher level than I could have on my own. Without God's perspective, I would have been intimidated by Bosworth."

Frustrated by the loss, he nevertheless felt an overwhelming sense of victory as he headed for the locker room. It was truly an opportunity for character enrichment.

"And I thought, what a climax to a great regular season. And in life, if I have ever faced anything in the business world, it hasn't been as intimidating as Brian Bosworth."

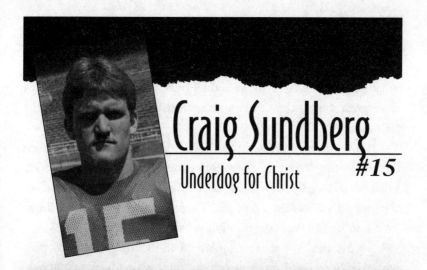

Craig Sundberg
Underdog for Christ
#15

Three-year letterman at quarterback

He considered himself an average NCAA Division I quarter-back. The hometown ballplayer followed one of his school's best-ever all-around signal callers. This athlete's statistics would leave no legacy. However, his name and final performance would be pen-ciled alongside some of his top contemporaries.' And this soft spo-ken individual would claim no personal glory in the accomplish-ment.

After playing in obscurity on the scout team and in the shadow of his predecessor, three-time All-Big Eight quarterback Turner Gill, the Lincoln Southeast graduate earned the starting reins for the 1984 campaign. Fifth-year senior Craig Sundberg's moment had arrived, but it would be an arduous one.

In the season's early weeks, Sundberg directed Nebraska to a 3 -0 record and a No. 1 ranking. The Husker offense outscored early nonconference opponents, including the eighth-ranked UCLA Bruins, by an average of 35 points. Sundberg's final year appeared to be promising.

"My senior season, from a playing standpoint, was a real roller coaster year," Craig recalled. "I started out as the heir apparent, following in Turner Gill's shoes and all of that. The first three games were great, but in the third game against UCLA I hurt my [right] shoulder.

"I just basically bruised the shoulder bone. It was right before the end of the first half. I threw a pass out of bounds down the left sidelines and a guy hit me just after I threw it. And as I landed on the ground, he was on top of me. There was a soreness there for at least four or five weeks, until I got it back to full strength.

"In the next game we traveled to the Carrier Dome to play unranked Syracuse. I was able to play, but I wasn't back to 100 percent. Nobody played well, including myself. We made a lot of mistakes and got beat [17-9]. My shoulder really took a beating in that game.

"I felt like I could play above the injury, but in reality it affected me. I didn't want to accept that something like that was going to keep me from playing after four years of waiting. But it did. And if nothing else, I would be thinking about it and it would cause me to kind of be timid at times.

"The next week was the Big Eight opener against Oklahoma State and I probably played the worst first half of football, maybe ever. I threw three interceptions. Backup junior quarterback Travis [Turner] came in toward the end of the first half and played the rest of the game. He got the starting nod the next game and then it was basically his job to lose his position as the starter."

Though admittedly frustrated, Sundberg attempted to keep a positive attitude.

"That was tough, after waiting on the sidelines for four years. But I tried to keep an eternal perspective on it, as best I could. That was usually easier said than done."

Coach Osborne encouraged him to hang in there, regardless of circumstances.

"During the middle of the season, I felt like, 'Lord, is this the way it's going to end? I've waited four years and I got to start at the beginning of the season. But is this it?'

"Because I didn't know from one week to the next. I seriously didn't know if I was ever going to play another down. Because after Travis came in and played well enough and really earned the right to be the starter, it was a week-by-week deal [to know who would start]. Basically, I didn't play much at all until the Oklahoma game.

"Probably the lowest of the lows was the Colorado game."

On October 20 in Boulder, he and Turner alternated playing time on the field for two-thirds of the contest. But the junior faired the better and held fast to the starting role following the 24-7 win.

"I'm not the type of person that would ever quit. But, if there was ever a time that I was close to it, just feeling like throwing the towel in, it would have been right after that game."

His faith and desire to honor God motivated him to persevere.

"Just knowing that God was in control kept me from quitting. It's like in Proverbs 3:5-6. Regardless of the situation, if you trust Him with all your heart, He's going to direct your paths. And it's going to be Him who is getting the glory."

Going into the final regular season game, Sundberg's shoulder healed back to normal and he saw more playing time behind Turner.

Ironically, on November 17, Turner endured his share of frustration as well. With a national championship berth on the line, the No. 1 Cornhuskers' 1984 title hopes vanished in a 17-7 loss to fourth-ranked Oklahoma in Lincoln.

"I know he was really down in the dumps at the end of the season because of the note that it ended on."

And those shared anxieties of striving to be the No. 1 player served as a source of common ground, uniting the two competitors.

"Travis and my friendship really blossomed right toward the last month of football."

The pair were already bonded in Christ as fellow believers, yet until late in the season, Craig maintained a polite distance.

"I think the first reason for that would have been just the fact that there was so much riding on being competitors for the same position. It was almost like you didn't want to let your guard down, too much. It was a healthy rivalry. We got along and everything outside of football. It wasn't like there was any hidden agenda or anything like that. It was just the idea that only one guy basically plays that position.

"But now I can think back and honestly be glad he came in and had the opportunities he had to start. But at the time, I wanted to be in there playing. Because as it turned out, he played very little his senior year. I wouldn't have said this at the time, but now I can look back on my anxieties during the '84 season, because of how trivial they were. Now it's not nearly as big of a deal. I'm glad he got the chance to play. Playing time-wise, his time was very limited. He had a knee injury during spring football season."

On January 1, 1985 Craig Sundberg had one more opportunity to play lead. The Lincolnite had earned the right to start in the Sugar Bowl against 12th-ranked Louisiana State.

But on New Year's Eve, his thoughts were far from football. The 6-foot-1, 190-pound senior shed approximately seven pounds that night while suffering a severe case of the flu. After a frustrating regular season, Sundberg was truly at the lowest point of his athletic career.

A small group of committed Christians from the team met privately to pray for the quarterback.

"I was sick. I mean it was bad. I don't know that I have ever been as sick. Afterwards I was told that they were very much lifting me up in prayer.

"I was so sick, that even though there were small feelings of being disappointed of maybe not being able to play, that I just didn't care—only that I would get better and feel better."

He managed only two hours of sleep prior to the contest and was finally able to digest his food.

"Before the game, I think all I had was a little bit of soda and some saltines. I was able to get something down and have it stay down." He described his recovery as miraculous.

"Basically, by about 1:30 that afternoon of the game, I was touched by God in a mighty way and was healed to a point of being at least able to go out that night and perform."

Sundberg still started, but struggled early in the game.

"We weren't real sharp on offense. I remember on the first series, on the second play it was a counter sweep pass and I tripped over my feet and lost 5 yards."

Could it be a sign of what could be another disappointing performance? In reality, great things were yet to come that night.

The primed Louisiana State Tigers scored on their next two possessions to take a 10-0 lead early in the second quarter.

But a poised Sundberg fired Nebraska's first touchdown strike in return.

"It was a brand new play we put in. It was a play action pass."

Sundberg faked the hand off to I-back Doug Dubose and sprinted left behind his wall of blockers.

"Doug Dubose floated back off to the right. I came out to the left like it [the pass] was going to go down and out to the split end.

"I pump-faked and flipped my feet around real quick and threw the ball to Doug. We had a convoy of linemen that floated back and did their blocks and we scored on a 31-yard screen pass."

Nebraska claimed the lead midway through the second period as the quarterback scored on a 9-yard counter-sweep.

"Part of me was ecstatic [following the touchdown], but I didn't have a lot of extra energy, so I wanted to conserve as much as I could. I was going on God's strength the entire time and whatever adrenaline was there."

The Husker senior would fire two more TD passes to seal a 28-10 victory. On the night he wrapped up a four touchdown performance, going 10-of-15 through the air for 143 yards.

During the game's waning moments, sports information personnel informed him that he was being named the 1985 Sugar Bowl's Most Valuable Player.

As the MVP, Sundberg historically stood in elite company with four first-round professional football draft picks. Previous Sugar Bowl MVPs included 1982 Heisman Trophy winning running back Herschel Walker of Georgia (1981), future All-Pro NFL quarterback Dan Marino of Pittsburgh (1982), national championship signal caller Todd Blackledge of Penn State (1983), and 1985 Heisman winner and two-sport star running back Bo Jackson of Auburn (1984).

"I was standing on the sidelines before the game was over and was told that I was the MVP. That's when God was preparing me for what would transpire in the next hour or two, with all the media and the press."

At the press conference, Sundberg related how God had worked in his life that night and through a disheartening senior season. He explained how the Lord healed him from the flu and enabled him to play the best game of his career.

"I could have given all the pat old answers, but that thought never entered my mind. I felt like God had exalted me to a position of being able to give Him the glory and the credit. I remember looking at some of the reporters faces. The gist of all their questions was, 'Craig, you're a fifth-year senior, you have waited behind Turner Gill for three years now, you end your season on this great deal—this has got to be the pinnacle of your career or your life! Tell us how you're feeling.'

"And I'd say the last thing they expected to hear was, 'Let me tell you what happened these last 16 hours.' I told the story, I don't know how many dozens of times. Basically, the end result of the game was it provided an opportunity to really give God the glory and Him all the credit for what had transpired that evening in the game. I felt His anointing from about two o'clock that afternoon until about two in the morning by the time I got back to the hotel."

And a well-earned rest was definitely in order.

"I don't know if I have ever been as tired, before or since then. I slept more the next three or four days than I did maybe for a few weeks after that."

And though tired, the former underdog found the energy to smile in reflection.

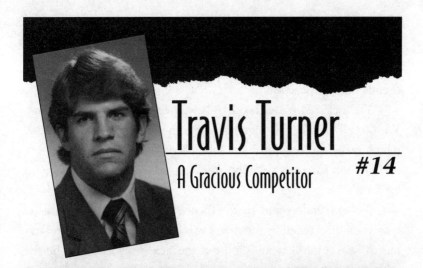

Travis Turner
A Gracious Competitor
#14

Gracious and competitive are not synonymous terms, but they blend well together in describing the character of a certain walk-on quarterback. Travis Turner was a 6-foot-3 signal caller from Scottsbluff, Neb. who would spend his final two seasons battling for and losing the starting job.

It was spring practice in 1984. Lincoln native senior Craig Sundberg was the projected heir apparent as three-time All-Big Eight option specialist Turner Gill finished his eligibility. The junior from western Nebraska had earned a scholarship and worked his way into the No. 2 spot.

Propelled by a message from former Husker All-American running back Jeff Kinney at a Fellowship of Christian Athletes meeting that winter, Turner said he focused on getting his spiritual life in order.

"I decided to get my life in a better place with the Lord," he explained. "That spring it really started making a difference because I was a lot more free from pressure. I went out to play and enjoy myself. I was very content and grateful just to be on the team, and really just having a chance to participate. And for the first time, I started seeing good fruit from that."

Fruit abounded as he was elevated from walk-on status and onto second team. Turner described how he and Sundberg became friends during the season.

"We lockered by each other. It was very friendly competition. We played racquetball together and other things besides football which made our relationship a lot closer."

Though sincerely friendly, Sundberg admittedly kept his guard up for a time.

"I could understand that," Turner sympathized, "because he was more threatened by me than I was by him. I wasn't the one trying to save a job. I would find out the next year just how he felt when I was the starter."

Meanwhile on the field, Nebraska cruised to a 3-0 record and solidified a No. 1 ranking with a 42-3 road win over eighth-rated UCLA.

But Sundberg suffered a shoulder injury against the Bruins and would struggle to return to top form for the remainder of the regular season. The capitol city native aggravated the joint during a 17-9 upset to unranked Syracuse in the Carrier Dome. Turner eventually took over as the starter midway through the schedule.

"I started against Missouri. It was hard for me because I knew how much it hurt Craig. He didn't take it badly. But it was difficult for me to watch because he had waited four years to start. It was bittersweet for me."

But just as success isn't necessarily a finality, the tall quarterback from Scottsbluff dropped to No. 2 again behind a healthy Sundberg. That slip followed a frustrating 10-point loss to fourth-ranked Oklahoma in Lincoln. The blemish ended then No. 1 Nebraska's bid for a national championship.

Travis continued to be supportive of the senior signal caller as the team prepared for a New Years Day contest with Louisiana State in New Orleans.

Adversity continued for Sundberg, however, as January 1st drew near. The upperclassman's shoulder had healed, but a severe bout with the flu on New Years Eve caused him to lose nearly eight pounds only hours before game time.

But Sundberg miraculously recovered. His condition improved enough to allow him to start, and even shine, as he passed for three touchdowns and rushed for one in sparking a 28-10 victory over LSU.

"Craig won back the starting job after the Oklahoma game," Turner noted. "He started the Sugar Bowl and won the MVP and I was grateful to be a part of it. It was a difficult year for Craig and God really honored his faithfulness."

Several months later, Travis Turner was the senior quarterback in a similar position. He would face his share of injuries as well as a permanent loss of the starting role.

A re-injury to a torn anterior cruciate ligament during the 1985 spring game hampered him for the remainder of his career. After having it scoped, Turner worked diligently in rehabilitation. But a herniated disc in his back suffered while weight lifting proved detrimental.

"Between my back and my knee during my senior year it wasn't very healthy. Confidence wasn't very good. And as fall practice started, I was still the starter. My speed was definitely not what it had been. They were trying to save me and not allow me to scrimmage. I wasn't very sharp and as a result, [redshirt sophomore quarterback] McCathorn Clayton was getting all the reps. He was getting better. And in the mean time, physically I wasn't operating very well."

In the end, Clayton earned the starting job for the remainder of the year.

Though frustrated by his decline and not particularly close to the surrounding quarterback competition, Turner opted to make the most of an opportunity.

"I really struggled, but God taught me a lot through it. I specifically remember the Lord convicting me to pray for him [Clayton] and that he does well and start helping him. That really became my focus. I was just praying for Mac [McCathorn Clayton] and wanting God to bless him and it just softened my heart. I gave him some insights I had. And the same for [freshman] Steve Taylor, I just did my best to encourage those guys and be supportive.

"There were times when my confidence was low. I remember asking [offensive guard and captain] Stan Parker for needed prayer. He not only prayed for me, but he also encouraged me on and off the playing field.

"I would tape my wrist and put some verse on it to encourage me, especially early in the year. I saved those pieces of tape and ran across those recently. It was something I really needed."

Travis Turner finished the year as a backup. And that being

frustrating enough, a nagging knee injury did not make the situation any easier.

"The knee was locking up on me. That cartilage would catch and literally lock my knee at an angle. I didn't tell coach Osborne because I knew he wouldn't play me. Physically, I was a mess.

"I was put in a role of mopping up and being a relief pitcher. I spent the next couple weeks trying to encourage Mac."

The backup eventually required reconstructive surgery following the regular season.

"I had surgery right after the Oklahoma game, so that was it for me."

The Huskers dropped their last two games, losing 27-7 to the Sooners at Norman and 27-23 to Michigan in the Jan. 1, 1986 Fiesta Bowl. Nebraska wrapped up a 9-3 season, finishing 10th in the UPI rankings and 11th in AP.

The quarterback from Scottsbluff stood on crutches along the sidelines during his team's loss to the Wolverines in Tempe, Arizona. Though it had been a frustrating year, it was not in vain. The season was truly character building as well as being one of opportunity.

"God did a lot of things. He softened my heart toward Mac and he gave me a platform. I was speaking at schools, churches, football banquets, and things like that continually. My wife Carol and I travelled around the whole state of Nebraska. And I got to share at the FCA breakfast at the Fiesta Bowl."

A year earlier, Travis had also taken advantage of opportunities to share his faith. Following their 1985 Sugar Bowl win, he and other Christian teammates banded together to share their faith in towns across the Big Red state. The small corps of players dubbed themselves Cornhuskers for Christ. They spoke wherever they could, whether in churches or public schools.

"We went to Kearney and spoke at the Holiday Inn in front of a group. We went to some classrooms in a couple of small public schools. Most of us spoke frequently at churches, FCA events, and at midget football banquets. It was nice that we were all together and getting a chance to share our faith, together. And that really was fun. Those are memories that we will always cherish."

Turner said he and teammate John Nichols also participated in a crusade in Scottsbluff, Neb.

"We went back to my hometown and spoke at my high school. It was fun having John and I together. John would tell stories and then all of these kids crowded around."

Though those times were special, Travis said it has disturbed him how people would put athletes on such a pedestal.

"In hindsight, it's kind of ironic that our credibility was based on the fact that we could play football. It wasn't based on maturity or understanding of scripture or being able to apply God's Word. It was mostly based on the fact that we were football players. It's ironic how we put athletes on a pedestal and give them instant credibility because they are athletes. And that's not necessarily the way to qualify somebody's character.

"It is interesting how we look for men who are able to share the gospel, rather than look for faithful men. I spent two years ministering to athletes in Phoenix and recognized the backwardness of that."

Turner added that he is very supportive of ministries directed to athletes. But it has bothered him when those Christian athletes are lifted up and looked to for leadership, when they may need to mature spiritually themselves.

"I'm glad they [ministries] are trying to reach people through the medium of sports. But I think they need to be careful not to put athletes in a leadership position before they are ready."

Travis expressed how his brother poured himself into his life, from a spiritual standpoint. Tim, a helicopter pilot in Vietnam and

scholarship football player at Colorado State, was the second oldest of the six siblings. Travis' elder by 15 years, Tim took him under
his wing at an early age as sort of a spiritual mentor. Thus, Travis
became a Christian at age nine after going forward at an altar call.
But he never took his relationship with God seriously until college.

"I didn't think too much about God. But Tim was always sort
of a looming presence on my life. He wanted me to get my life
right. And I probably just never heeded his help and correction. His
prayers and determination to encourage me had a huge impact.

"During my senior year at Nebraska, he worked out with me
and was the one who really believed in me. He trained me and
taught me how to throw and really believed in me. He took me to
church. He shared the Word with me and challenged me. He certainly didn't hide his faith in terms of the way he shared it with me.
I think Vietnam had a lot to do with strengthening his faith."

At the university, Travis futilely sought fulfillment in athletics.
But as a junior, the message by former Nebraska All-American running back Jeff Kinney helped him to refocus his priorities back
toward God.

"I was trying to save my life through football and thought it
would bring me happiness. But, in the process, I was really not at
peace and not at a good place with God. That was at a time when
Jeff Kinney spoke at our huddle group in Lincoln. I then made
another conscientious step toward the Lord and discipled myself.
That spring I just had a lot more peace in my heart."

And through the highs and lows of his last two football
seasons, he began to grasp God's perspective on what was truly
important in his life.

"One of the biggest things I learned was that God's vision and
purpose for our lives is a lot bigger than ours is. He's not wrapped
up in worldly success. He's truly interested in building our character. And if we can find that in our circumstances, then we can grow.

But if we're constantly looking at the circumstance or the score, then we are going to miss out on His blessings."

And through learning that truth, Travis Turner became a gracious competitor.

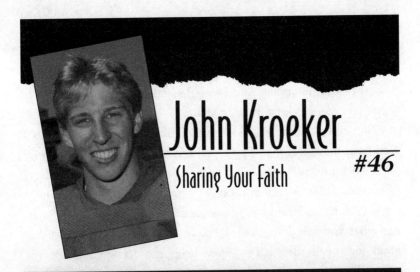

John Kroeker

Sharing Your Faith

#46

Academic All-American punter 1988, three-year letterman 1986-88

He was the pride of his hometown. The quiet, blond, blue-eyed youth of a small Mennonite community in southeast Nebraska finished high school in 1984 as the state's best all-around athlete and was bound for the University of Nebraska on a football scholarship. A diligent student-athlete, he scored the second highest total career points in national high school football history at 672 and was an all-stater on the basketball court. An honor student, he graduated from Henderson High with a 3.94 grade point average. John Kroeker responded to the challenges before him, whether in the classroom or on the field, with noteworthy results. Reared in a small Bible-believing community, he admitted he was sheltered from many every day stresses of teenage life. His Christian faith would be stretched at the collegiate level.

As the Cornhuskers' sophomore punter, an older teammate confronted him on the need to share that faith with others. Ken Kaelin, a senior starting fullback from Westerville, Neb. provided sincere spiritual tutelage for the younger athlete.

"I specifically remember Ken Kaelin taking me under his wing and he said, 'John, you need to get involved.'" Kroeker recalled. "He taught me how to share my faith. He got asked to speak at a lot of different FCA functions. And he started taking me along. He said, 'John, you have to learn how to share.'

"I'm sure I stumbled and bumbled along the first few times I went with him. But it really helped me to learn how to share my faith. Then once you do start sharing your faith, there's a high level of accountability. When you publicly profess things, it puts you in a whole different realm where people's eyes are on you and watching what you are doing and if you're walking the talk. That was great for me. It definitely helped keep me accountable for my actions."

Kroeker embraced that faith as a sophomore in high school, but only after being slightly prodded. Similar to Ken Kaelin's friendly confrontation toward him at the university level, Kroeker desired spiritual leadership as a teenager. As a youth he had been saturated with Christianity his whole life, but he wanted someone to personally confront him with the gospel message before he felt he could accept it.

"My father came down to my bedroom downstairs. He never came downstairs unless I was in trouble or something. And he just said, 'John, are you a Christian?'

"And I said, 'No, but I'd like to [become one] tonight if you would do that with me.'

"And it really shocked him, because he just made the assumption that I was. That wasn't the answer that he was looking for. So we prayed together and I just asked God into my heart, to be the Lord of my life. There was no lightning flash or wind blowing through the the room or anything," John laughed. "There was just a great peace."

John explained that his eldest brother previously voiced concern to their father about his salvation.

"My dad just got off the phone with my oldest brother who was concerned with my salvation. And he asked my dad to visit with me about it. Dad didn't want to do it. And my brother said, 'Just ask. Just find out where he's at.'

"He had been praying for me. I don't know why he had been, but God had definitely been moving. So don't take anything for granted and don't underestimate the power of prayer. Be praying for people."

During his latter collegiate seasons John grew from being a follower to being a spiritual leader. Kroeker said he appreciated the positive examples of a handful of upperclassmen.

"The Ken Kaelins of the world, [offensive linemen] Stan Parker, Mike Hoeffler, and Brad Johnson were some really committed Christians. They were two years older than me. After those guys graduated I tried to be the person to encourage the younger players. Because I had seen the older guys model encouragement, it was much easier for me to become an encourager myself."

As an upperclassman he sought out opportunities to share his faith, using his tie to Nebraska football as a platform.

"There weren't that many outspoken Christians on the team. If anyone asked for a football player to share at an event, my name came up quite often–granted, being a punter is not the glamour position. I thank God that he did give me that platform and I had many opportunities to share. There weren't too many weeks when I wasn't sharing my testimony or speaking at a school.

"In today's society, the athlete is put up on a pedestal and wrongly so. But it was really neat for kids to see that there is another side of football."

Kroeker matured on the field as well as off. He defined his priorities during his three-year career as the starting punter. By nature of the position, he saw limited playing time and felt somewhat disenchanted. Thus he committed himself to improving upon that one skill and to contributing to the overall team effort.

"Punting is pretty much a repetition thing. There are a lot of little small intricacies [to concentrate on]. It's kind of like a golf game, it doesn't take too much to have a bad strike on the ball. I was out there every day punting about a 100 balls a day."

And though he says his career stats were average, he said he cherished those memories and the opportunity it gave to share his faith.

"I really think God called me there to play football. And as it turned out, I had a fairly mediocre career, I mean it was nothing great. During my three years of punting, I averaged 40.0. And if you ask a punter what he wants to average, he would say 40 yards. But I really saw that it was the people, the relationships and the lives that I was able to impact through the platform of Nebraska football that I had. I do feel that I was in God's will even though I didn't achieve the athletic success that I wanted. I do feel used by God and don't feel bad about that."

The former punter said life must be viewed from God's eternal perspective rather than from one based upon personal gratification.

"God is more concerned about our holiness than He is about our happiness. It seems like we're always concerned about our circumstances instead of His Kingdom. If you take a look at the right perspective, what He is trying to teach you and what you can learn in whatever situation or scenario you are going through, that's what He's looking for. He's looking to see in what way you are going to respond. Are you going to respond in a Christ-like manner? That's what I learned through the trials, temptations and struggles of big-time football and going to college and actually getting out in the real world, too."

That attitude did not go unnoticed by his peers. During a road trip from a charity basketball game for seniors he realized how closely some had been observing him.

"Sometimes you don't know what kind of impact your life has on people. On one of the trips I was the only Christian in that van and we were coming back from a game. And one of the guys just started talking about spiritual things and I got to share my faith.

"And my teammate just said, 'John, you're one guy that I really respect. It appears that you walk the talk.' You could just tell that there was just a lot of questioning of the lifestyle and what Christ meant to me in my life. And the whole group in that van had pretty much the same consensus that there was something that I had that was different. There was a peace about me. There was an assurance there. The Bible talks about earning the respect of both the Christian and the non-Christian. I really felt good about that trip knowing that I wasn't just here playing football, there were five years that were invested into the lives of fellow players. Hopefully those were seeds that were planted that someone else can reap further down the road."

The Henderson native may have played an average university football career, but it was one in which a once sheltered shy young man sought to honor God with what abilities he had.

The 1990s
Building a dynasty

Three-straight national championship games and two consecutive NCAA titles highlight an era of dominance built following seven straight bowl losses. A revamped defense, overpowering offensive lines, great skill players, overall perfection, and even spiritual revival earmarked this corps of players. Along with their predecessor, the 1971 Husker squad, the 1995 Nebraska football team has ranked among the greatest college football teams ever assembled. No opponent ever posed a serious threat in beating the 1995 national champions.

But the fading brilliance of trophies in light of eternity was evidenced with the sudden death of former quarterback Brook Berringer on April 18, 1996. Berringer had enjoyed both the role of starter and endured watching on the sidelines during the championship seasons. But far greater than his football skills was his proven character and relationship with the Creator. The native of northwestern Kansas played courageously in a handful of games while suffering from a collapsed lung. Though he was admittedly frustrated at times, he was not shaken. As a senior, he said his new-found faith in God brought him peace and hope.

"During my whole career I've been on both ends of the spectrum," said the late Berringer, prior to the Jan. 2, 1996 national championship game. "I've enjoyed the starting position and I've had to suffer through the frustrations of not getting to play at all. But, you know, through this whole ordeal I have been able to use my faith as something that is just a complete comfort.

"It's just amazing, the difference that it's made in my life. I know where I'm headed, the ultimate goal and it brings everything into perspective. And it makes football, although it is a big part of my life, something that is not as important as maybe I once thought. And it really prioritizes things in my life."

And Brook's passing has continued to illuminate those priorities to many others was well.

Trev Alberts

Perspective of a Gamer

#34

1993 Butkus Award winner, Consensus All-American outside linebacker 1993, First Team All-Big Eight 1992-1993 NCAA Top Six Award Winner, Academic All-American 1993, Academic All-Big Eight 1991-93, 1993 NU defensive captain, four-year letterman 1990-93

He has been described as a one-man wrecking crew.

He is Trev Alberts.

The 6-foot-4, 240-pound 1993 Butkus Award winner and Academic All-American sacked opposing quarterbacks a school record 15 times for minus 88 yards during that regular season. He dropped Heisman trophy winner Charlie Ward of Florida State three times for losses during the Jan. 1, 1994 National Championship Orange Bowl.

The Cedar Falls, Iowa native grinned as he described that thrill of toppling an opposing quarterback.

"As a defensive player, and specifically as a outside linebacker-defensive end, it's the best feeling there is. Beating your offensive tackle is a struggle all day, he's a big guy. And then, once you get past him, you have the running back. And so, once you get past those guys your eyes really light up because you get a free shot on the quarterback. And that's really the reward for an outside line-backer."

Honored by *Football News* as the nation's top defensive player, he played for the nation's highest ranked undefeated team. The 1993 Huskers did not always play pretty, yet they found ways to win throughout the regular season. An example was against unranked Kansas when Nebraska survived a two-point conversion attempt in the game's waning moments to cling to a one-point victory.

Nebraska's 1993 squad was comprised of overachievers. Those players stood bonded in spirit and purpose. Yet they were smirked at by the national media. They were the ugly ducklings. Going into the Orange Bowl, their opponent, top-ranked Florida State, was favored by 17-and-a-half points.

"We went into that game with no respect," Trev stressed. "The week preceding, I remember going to all the activities with the players on the other team and you could just tell that they felt like, 'Why do we have to come down here and play these jokers? This isn't even going to be a close game.' And we never said a word. They were saying different things and we just took it all in and used it to motivate us.

"In 1993 we used all that stuff to our advantage. Coach Osborne kind of helped teach us not to let those things hinder us, but rather grab onto them and use them as energy and use them to help motivate us. I think that's what we did. We just said, 'Hey, keep it coming. That's just what we need. We need more stuff just to fuel the fire and make us more determined to win ball games.' "

Ignited, Nebraska often dominated both sides of the ball with seasoned confidence. The Huskers limited the nation's most potent offense to 18 points and even led the game in total offense, possession time, third-down conversions, and in sacks recorded. Yet, with 15 seconds left in the fourth quarter, Nebraska was trailing by two points and searching for a miracle.

Alberts stood on the sidelines with his elbow in a cast. His joint

still felt the effects of a dislocation injury suffered against Oklahoma only five weeks earlier. He focused on his team's offense on the field, steadfast in hope.

Only moments earlier, Seminole freshman kicker Scott Bentley drilled a 22-yard field goal for the lead, culminating a 65-yard drive in 55 seconds. That scoring strike came on the heels of a 27-yard field goal by NU's Byron Bennett's with 1:16 remaining.

The outside linebacker held his head high, but it disturbed him that he didn't make that needed big play on defense to stop FSU. Alberts watched helplessly as his roommate's 45-yard field goal attempt sailed wide left at the gun. The final score, Florida State 18, Nebraska 16.

"You wait all your life for a chance to kick the winning field goal and it just didn't happen," Bennett said following the game. "I think maybe God has something better for me in life."

Alberts was philosophical as well.

"I feel like we're still champions," he stated at the contest's conclusion. "There's not a frown on my face."

He recalled coach Osborne's words in the locker room.

"I'll never forget coach Osborne saying that if you get a group of guys together and if they play up to their capabilities, that's all he'll ever ask. And he told us we played well enough to win that game.

"Now there's intangibles, things that you don't have any control over that can happen. And those things, unfortunately, just seemed to happen to us that day. But I didn't walk out there with my head down, I felt like as a group everybody gave what they had. And I think that's what athletics is all about—you're going to win, you're going to lose, and effort is the main thing.

"But I would have to say that if there's one thing about my college career that haunts me in some way, I would have to say it's that final drive," he said with a hint of irritation in his voice. "There's been times when I will still dream about it. Especially right after it happened, I had a great career and won a lot of awards, but the one series of downs where I had to step up and make a play, when it was on the line, I didn't produce. And regardless of what I had done before that, if I had ten sacks before that in that game, it didn't make any difference. And that bothered me."

The biggest game of his life behind him, the highly decorated collegian left Nebraska with a degree in speech communications and a job in the National Football League. Indianapolis selected him as the fifth player chosen overall in the 1994 draft.

And with all the accolades, Alberts stressed that his parents have helped him keep the honors and even the frustrations in perspective. He credited them for shaping his values in life.

"I have an outstanding set of support people, including my parents, who are quick to bring me down to reality if I begin to act too prideful. The Bible warns us to keep from being too prideful. I try to take that attitude to heart. It's not easy to be humble for most athletes, but I believe it's important for any athlete to keep from being too self-absorbed.

"My parents mean the world to me," he added. "They brought me up in a Christian home. I remember sitting in church every Sunday morning, Sunday night and Wednesday night. It was the central theme of our family. And my parents have brought me up in a Christian home and raised me with the right values. And I feel that I just owe them a tremendous debt and I hope that I will be able to pay them back."

The sturdy defensive end reflected on the close relationship with his father. Their bond developed through the elder's loving discipline.

"I have an interesting relationship with my dad. When I was young, I went through some stages of obvious rebellion at about 12 and 13-years-old. And my dad was really a disciplinarian and believed in doing things the right way. There was no slacking off with him–hard work was very important to him. I received my share of discipline, and at times, it wasn't easy to accept."

But the struggles proved worthwhile as the father-son bond only tightened while Trev was away at UNL.

"Every week I got a letter from my dad for five years without a miss. I still have got every one of those letters. He's like a best friend to me. I can tell him anything, he respects me and I respect him. It's just a great relationship. And more than anything else, my dad stands up for his family over anything. He will only put God in front of his family. In the world that we live in, that's the thing that I respect the most about him."

And it was that spiritual foundation that both Ken and Linda Alberts laid in the home that prepared Trev to accept Christ while in grade school.

"When I was only six years old, I recall being concerned about going to heaven when I died. In church they used to talk about hell, the lake of fire, and those sort of things and it really frightened me. And, so when I tried to talk to my parents about it, at first, they were, 'Well, Trev's a little too young to probably know what really is going on.'

"But I think every parent should be sensitive to children when it comes to spiritual things. The Bible even says that it's that simple that they can understand. At six years old I knew that something had to happen or I was going to go to hell. When I was eight years old on November 7, 1978, my dad was gone, he was on a business trip. And I asked my mom if she would read some Bible verses to me and she read a few gospel tracts and went through quite a few verses in the Bible and just stopped with John 6:47, 'Verily, verily I say unto you, he that believes on me has everlasting life.' And she went on and read a few more. I knew all the popular Bible verses, John 3:16 and Romans 10:9 and everything, and after all those things, I just kind of realized for the first time that nothing I could do merited my salvation. There wasn't anything that I had to do. I mean, God didn't ask me to give him a million dollars. I didn't have to buy it. He didn't ask me to try to live a good life and maybe I would get to heaven. He simply said that He sent His Son. And all I had to do was repent and accept the fact that Jesus died on the cross and that His blood was enough to bring me to heaven. And at that time, it just came to me that all I needed to do was rest on the fact that when He died, He died for me as well. And I just accepted the fact that He died for me, and ever since, it's just been wonderful knowing your sins are forgiven. It gives you a real peace and joy that, I guess, the people that aren't Christians, don't really have."

And that relationship with his Savior translated into an intensity on the field. The linebacker illustrated his perspective of a gamer.

"You think about how Jesus might have played football and I

guarantee you he would have been one of the most intense, hardest players on the team and never quit. And when I look at what things Jesus Christ went through in His life, a lot of the things I go through seem pretty small. So He's a pretty incredible example to try to follow."

In July 1997, Albert's announced his retirement from the NFL after three years of nagging injuries. The dislocated elbow injury suffered in college caused him to miss much of his '94 rookie season. Shoulder dislocation injuries hampered him over his final two seasons. Though his career was short and painful, Trev had no regrets.

"It was a wonderful experience and I would do it again. Sometimes we think we have all the answers and have our plans set out. Sometimes our plans aren't someone else's plans. The NFL wasn't for me and that was OK. I really felt fortunate to even play football in college and enjoy success and be able to experience the NFL. I have no regrets. I don't look back. There isn't anything I would've done differently."

But 1993's top collegiate linebacker has not left football completely behind him. The former All-American has embarked on a sports broadcasting career. His on-air regiment includes spending weekends as an analyst for *CNN/Sports Illustrated,* among other on-air reporting. A family man, he and his wife Angela and their son Chase reside in Lincoln, Neb.

John Parrella

A Lesson in Maturity

#92

**All-Big Eight defensive tackle 1991-92,
1992 NU defensive captain,
three-year letterman 1990-92**

The committed family man and fierce bulldog of the San Diego Charger defensive front lines has displayed a maturity that was kindled after his temporary expulsion from the University of Nebraska.

Following months of reckless partying and allowing his grade point average to plummet below a 2.0, the sophomore found himself as an ex-student and former football player. His parents were furious. His girlfriend was displeased. His coaches were unimpressed. And he wanted to change.

"I can honestly remember praying, 'Lord, help me get back into school.'" John Parrella recalled. "The university helped me get back into school. Of course, I had to go back and talk to the chancellor. And coach Osborne said, 'Look, we're going to give you one more chance.'"

The consumer science major did raise his grades just enough, but with little effort and minimal class attendance. Defensive coordinator Charlie McBride was not impressed with his half-hearted attitude.

"One day I remember Charlie McBride grabbed me and said, 'If you ever want to see the green grass at Memorial Stadium, I don't care how good of a football player you are, you have to go to school.'

"We had quite a few great offensive linemen in college, and McBride used to say to me, 'Is their heart pumping blood or Kool-Aide? Are they just full of ability and no heart?!'"

The defensive tackle and Grand Island, Neb. native then committed himself to academics and football, yet his spiritual life was still not a priority. Thus, his longtime girlfriend, Leigh, gave him an ultimatum to change.

"My wife now, my girlfriend then, grabbed me and said, 'We need to change.'

"She was a Christian, already, and so was I, but we weren't living it. And she said, 'Look, if you want a relationship with me, we both have got to change.'"

Parrella did not appreciate the confrontation at the time.

"I almost felt like I didn't even want to be around her any more because she wanted to do something that I didn't want."

But the stress from his temporary expulsion and pressure from those he cared about continued to weigh upon him until he finally broke.

"It just got to the point where I couldn't take any more and I said, 'Lord, help me out here. This is stupid. I need to do something.'

"It just seemed like overnight, wham! It just happened. My attendance in school and my grades went way up. On the football field I went from a guy who was probably one of the laziest players to a guy where they couldn't slow me down. I just started going nuts. It just seemed like everything clicked."

John's spiritual life clicked as well, directly impacting his play on the field.

"I had a pastor at the university, who was with Campus Crusade for Christ. I asked him, 'If Jesus played football, what would He be like?'

"And he said, 'He would be the hardest player to ever play the game. He would be the hardest hitter. He would be the biggest, the fastest and the strongest. From the snap to the whistle he would go full speed.'

"And I thought, that's how I wanted to be. And be clean and not play dirty."

For his on-field accomplishments, Parrella was named All-Big Eight following his junior and senior seasons. As a senior defensive captain, he received league player of the week honors for his showing against the eighth-ranked Colorado Buffaloes on Halloween 1992. And Colorado was a team he resented.

As a high school senior at Grand Island Central Catholic, Parrella inked with the Buffaloes in February 1988. But Colorado reneged on their offer, accidently offering 24 scholarships, with only 22 to give. He then walked on to Nebraska.

"They called me up [in July] and said they had to take my scholarship away. Granted, they hurt me and embarrassed me, because of what happened. But they hurt my parents because they hadn't planned to pay for my college tuition. I always said to myself, if we ever play these guys, I'm just going to unleash something that they have never seen before."

As a junior in 1991, Parrella recorded one of two Husker sacks on a frigid night in Boulder. The 6-foot-5, 290-pound tackle was satisfied with his personal performance, but was let down by the 19-19 final score.

Colorado nose tackle Jeff Brunner surmised the feelings of both teams following the game.

"This was just like kissing your sister on a cold, cold, cold night," he said. "No satisfaction in that. But maybe a game like this should end up in a tie."

"I thought I played a great game," recalled Parrella, "but I was disappointed."

Things were quite different the next fall in Lincoln.

"My senior year," the defensive lineman said with satisfaction, "we beat them 52-7. I just wanted to run over to that sideline and look at their coaching staff and go, 'See what you lost out on. This could have been the other way around.'"

But Parrella kept his thoughts to himself and let his actions speak for themselves. He finished the game with eight tackles, including three sacks for 25-yards lost. He batted down one pass and hurried the Buffalo quarterbacks five times. One of those pressure moments led directly to an interception. Parrella and the Blackshirts stuffed the Buffalo ground game, holding them to only 8 rushing yards.

The tall defensive tackle later wrapped up the regular season with second team All-America honors and was chosen by Buffalo in the second round of the 1993 NFL draft. Acquired by San Diego as a free agent in 1994, the former Husker has played in two Super Bowls with both teams. But a favorite memory for the Charger lineman was beating the Steelers in the January 1995 American Football Conference Championship game.

It was Sunday, January 15 at Three Rivers Stadium in Pittsburgh. Parrella had been looking forward to an opportunity to start in a big NFL game for a long time. This was his second chance to play lead as a professional.

"I'm all fired up. I'm in my second NFL start. It's a big game, the game before the Super Bowl. I'm thinking, 'Okay, here we go, Lord. I can do all things through Christ who strengthens me.' "

But adversity struck early in the game.

"Second play—wham! I hit the ground. I break my thumb and split it in two.

"And I'm thinking, 'Now, Lord, why would You want this to happen? This is my second game ever and probably the best game I'm ever going to start in my life?'

"Well, I think He challenged me to see how bad I wanted to play football. Because in my rookie year at Buffalo I was at a point where I really didn't want to play.

"That experience helped me regain something I had lost, and that's the ability to play through pain. When I was in college, I didn't have a problem playing with pain. To some degree, every football player must play with some pain at the college or pro level.

"Before each play, I would think about a verse from the Bible like Philippians 4:13, 'I can do all things through Christ who strengthens me.' I prayed, 'Thank You for giving me the opportunity to play football and enjoy it.'"

Split thumb and all, Parrella finished that AFC title game with one solo tackle for a loss and two assists. He also played a role in breaking Pittsburgh's momentum during a key series late in the game.

The two minute warning had just expired and Pittsburgh trailed by four points. The Steelers lined up on Charger's 9-yard line on first down. The ball went to Steeler running back Barry Foster, who attempted to run off his left tackle. But the former Husker defensive lineman shut down the hole, stuffing Foster for negative yardage. Three plays later, Pittsburgh ran out of downs and San Diego ran out the clock. The final, Chargers 17, Steelers 13.

It was a different story for San Diego two weeks later. On January 29, a stocked 49er squad stomped the Chargers 49-26 in Super Bowl XXIX at Joe Robbie Stadium in Miami. It was Parrella's second NFL title game loss in a row as Buffalo fell to Dallas 30-13 the year before.

Though he did not start and his team was again soundly beaten, that game has been a positive source of reflection, he said.

"The Super Bowl that year was a great memory."

Big games have been fun and have their place for the stocky competitor. But honoring God as a responsible father and husband rated far and above on his priority list.

"Since we've had a child it seems it's even more important that we have Christ in our life, because we want to make sure that he receives Christ. We want to raise him in a Christian home. And that's harder than anything. That's harder than going out onto the football field."

He added that Christian teammates have been valuable in helping him to maintain a consistency in his spiritual life.

"The neatest thing is being held accountable by other guys on the team. There's just strength in numbers. It has just helped a lot. And it's a great feeling."

Maturing in his faith and in his priorities, Parrella has continued to thrive since that pivotal day at Nebraska when he nearly let his dreams slide. A vigorous commitment to honoring God has carried him far from the days when he was an undisciplined college student.

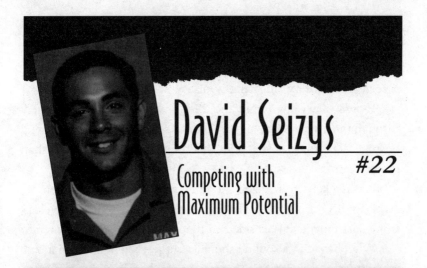

David Seizys
#22
Competing with Maximum Potential

**Special teams and backup wingback,
three-year letterman 1991-93**

David Seizys was a 5-foot-9 little known walk-on special teams player from Fort Calhoun High School in Seward, Neb. Yet, one image of him has embedded itself in Nebraska football history.

One second remained on the January 1, 1994 National Championship Orange Bowl clock. Husker kicker Byron Bennett lined up for the potential game winning 45-yard field goal. No. 22 reeled in the center snap and placed it for Bennett. The kick sailed wide left as the previously undefeated Cornhuskers fell to Florida State 18-16.

"Everyone had total confidence in Byron," the fifth-year kick holder recalled, shaking his head in frustration. "As the ball came back, I knew it was good. But the wind just took it. And as it drifted off, a Florida State player just killed me."

Seizys looked to the referee for a flag, but none was thrown.

"I laid back, put my hands over my eyes and just started crying. I knew it [our loss] was for a reason, but it just hurt.

"Not everything on earth is going to go the way you want it to," David affirmed with hopefulness in his voice. "God has His intentions.

"Reading 2 Corinthians 4:18 helped me deal with the loss. 'So we fix our eyes not on what is seen, but on what is unseen. For what is seen is temporary, but what is unseen is eternal.'"

Words of wisdom from the 22-year old athlete, but learned through the usual school of hard knocks and mistakes. A prolonged hospital stay three years prior had served to springboard that growth.

It was likely he realized the gravity of the moment when he awoke in his hospital bed. His tired eyes probably took in the electronic instruments on his side and the looks of his relieved parents.

What began as a routine shoulder surgery, culminated in a bad reaction to the anesthesia, he explained. And as a result, David slipped in and out of consciousness several times before fully awakening several hours later that night. Doctors later informed him that he could have slipped into a coma, he said.

"I wasn't getting enough oxygen to my brain, which could cause a comatose state. My oldest sister was yelling at me several times to breathe. It was really hard. At one point I was sick and tired of fighting. I just wanted to sleep. I probably could have slipped into a coma. It was scary. When I finally woke up that night, and was breathing normal, you could tell the feeling in the room was such a sense of relief."

David later reflected on his past two years in the Big Red. He had been obsessed with being a star but had found only injuries and disillusionment. Besides the shoulder problem, he had suffered minor recurring knee injuries since his senior season in high school. The backup receiver also was going nowhere on the Nebraska depth charts. It wasn't easy being a walk-on.

Seizys eventually recovered from the surgery as he resumed his active campus lifestyle. The underclassman partied to fit in and found himself drunk every weekend. He cut classes to sleep in following the night scene. His grades plummeted and he was put on academic probation.

"I got caught up in the football hoopla and partying. It was just a real ugly picture. School, football, and this great social life wasn't taking me anywhere."

David knew he needed to change his attitude and put forth more effort in the classroom. And he also felt the eyes of a Christian teammate upon him to just get his act together. But he continued to slide.

His head throbbed as he washed his hands following another weekend bash. David peered into the mirror. He didn't like what he saw.

"I felt like I didn't know who the person was in the reflection. I ran into my room and just started crying because all these things were no longer taking me anywhere. I started praying. I knew I needed to change."

He prayed that would God bring someone along who would help him straighten out his life. Tears filled his eyes as he sprawled across his bed and drifted off to sleep.

Hard rock music pounded the walls of the Husker weight room the next afternoon. David grimaced as he lifted the heavy dumbbell to his chest. It felt good to work out.

A man approached. David recognized him immediately from his hometown.

Rob Fitzgerald had graduated from Fort Calhoon High School a few years ahead of him. He was currently active with campus ministry work.

"How's school and football going?" he asked.

"Great," David lied. "I couldn't be happier with things right now."

Rob looked him in the eye.

"I'm going to go out on a limb, here," he smiled thoughtfully, "but, how's your walk with Jesus Christ?"

David was floored.

His prayers were answered. Fitzgerald would be the helper he had asked for.

The pair began a Bible study. Though he had grown up in a strong Christian home and said he had accepted Christ, David admitted he never made God a serious part of his life.

"Rob was really good with challenging me. I started getting personal in prayer with God. I didn't commit my life to Christ right away though."

But in March 1991 David prayed with Rob to rededicate his life to Christ.

"It was kind of a renewal; being recommitted after I had messed up so much."

With God as the guiding priority in his life, he committed himself to making some definite lifestyle changes.

"The biggest change was socially. I truly made an effort to step back from going to parties. I started becoming independent as a person, rather than wanting to be in the spotlight of the social world."

That fall he did not allow himself to be frustrated with any lack of progress on the team depth charts. Seizys turned his perspective to serving God in every circumstance.

"I started having fun in football again. I had an inner peace. I wasn't serving football any more. I was serving Christ. School started turning around. I started studying. I declared a math major and eventually elementary education. God was showing me what field I needed to get into. Socially, it wasn't important any more to go to parties. It was important who David Seizys should be for Christ."

The walk-on found a niche on special teams. He made the second unit punt return team and later started on the kickoff team. During his senior season he also held for PATs and field goals. His role wasn't glamorous, but it was a chance to contribute. And he took pride in it.

"God had given me another glorious position that nobody realizes is so important until the team loses by one point. It's not something that gets attention in the papers. But that's what I like. Because I can glorify God through the blue collar work that He has given me."

A favorite memory of this little-known special teamer happened during his final home game. It was Nov. 26, 1993 and the foe was 16th-ranked Oklahoma. No. 2 Nebraska was shooting for their first undefeated regular season and championship berth in a decade. Playing in below zero windchill, Nebraska scored a touchdown to break a 7-7 deadlock with 13:20 remaining in the game. On the ensuing kickoff, Oklahoma native Mike Minter forced a fumble which teammate David Seizys recovered on the Sooner 20. One play later, I-back Calvin Jones scored to put the game away. The final, Nebraska 21, Oklahoma 7.

"I recovered the fumble. And it was just such an awesome feeling when Calvin scored on the next play. That play was such a big play in sealing the game. I have to give a lot of credit to [freshman rover] Mike Minter because he caused the fumble. I thank God for that moment. That will be a play that I will remember for the longest time."

In late November 1991, David met another person who would profoundly impact his life. He befriended Kim Tonniges, a freshman middle blocker for the Lady Husker volleyball team.

"I knew she was a Christian. Looking back it was another person Christ brought along to straighten my life out. I was still struggling in my Christian walk. We started becoming close friends, but she didn't want to pursue a relationship unless she knew where I was with Christ. I told her I had recommitted my life to Christ. And she said, 'You don't have to say that just to please me.' And I explained to her what steps I had been taking. It was kind of a relief to her because she knew where I stood."

And though committed in his faith, David realized that there still were other areas in his life he needed to tie down. He also recognized he needed to be more bold in sharing that faith with others.

"She convicted me. She wouldn't pursue a relationship unless I walked with Christ. She played an important role in giving me a challenge as an infant in Christ. It was that challenge that made me realize that it isn't a one time commitment. It's a commitment every day."

Over two years later, they were married August 12, 1994.

And with a degree in hand, David has taught third and fourth graders at an elementary school in Lincoln.

Formerly an obscure special teams player in a large football program, Seizys has devoted himself to instilling that same enthusiasm into his young students—a desire for each one to maximize their God-given potential.

Tony Veland

In God's Hands

#9

Second team All-Big Eight free safety 1995,
1995 NU defensive captain,
three-year letterman 1992, 94-95

It was Sept. 11, 1993 at Memorial Stadium in Lincoln, Neb. and the backup quarterback was mopping up en route to a 50-27 blowout of Texas Tech. Tony Veland, a scholarship product of Omaha Benson High, kept the ball on an option play and rushed for the first down marker. A defender hit him low as he ruptured his right patellar tendon.

"It was a freak accident. I planted my foot and some guy grabbed me. My leg couldn't sustain it, so it just severed all the way across."

The injury not only sidelined him for the remainder of the season, but it also marked his last game as a quarterback. The relief signal caller's 15 rushing yards and one touchdown against the Red Raiders would be his final stats as an offensive player.

A broken collarbone in late August a year earlier caused him to miss the first five games of '92 and knocked him out of the starting role. His dreams within the confines of the gridiron were depleting fast. The frustration of the uncontrollable factors of athletics mounted upon the 20-year old engineering major. From time to time, the young quarterback probably still felt the pain of losing his father during his junior year in high school. Discouragement deepened within his heart.

But a letter of needed encouragement from an unknown fan would offer the spark his life needed to help him persevere.

Diane Yeutter was an elementary teacher in Lexington, Neb. who, along with her husband Ed, would regularly write Nebraska football players who appeared to need a lift. It was through her prayers and timely note that gave the college sophomore the ray of hope he needed.

"I was really low in my career. It was right after I tore my patellar tendon. It had to be the Lord speaking to her for her to write me, because she wrote me out of the blue. What she said in the letter pretty much captured the way that I felt at the time."

The note expressed genuine sympathy for his struggles and offered spiritual encouragement.

"She said that all things happen for a reason and that the Lord is working in my life. She told me that I may not enjoy what's going on right now, but that I need to thank the Lord because He has a bigger and better plan for me. And even though I don't understand it, I need to have faith because my life isn't in my hands anyway."

Those words were thought provoking. He knew only too well how the bitter disappointments of life can, at times, truly be out of any person's control. Mrs. Yeutter's letter planted a seed of searching for God within his heart. He began to correspond with this newfound friend as he persevered through the sidelining injury.

During the weeks that followed, the former prep two-way player also contemplated his status on the field. He decided to switch to defense.

"About a month or two after I tore my patellar tendon I figured I had so much bad luck at quarterback that I needed to try something different. When I was first being recruited to Nebraska, they had wanted me to play defensive back, anyway. So I figured I'd go ahead and give it a try."

Meanwhile, his teammates came within a missed field goal of winning the 1993 national title and hungrily sought a rematch the following year.

The 6-foot-2, 200-pound junior missed the entire spring practice season as he rehabilitated his right knee. Veland had

unfinished business in his personal athletic career as did his team. He was determined to come out strong in '94.

"It was really a great year. We had our motto, 'Unfinished Business' and I think everybody really had taken that personally. In the off season, it was really grueling and we worked really hard to better ourselves. Once the year started, we were pretty much ready for anything."

In the season opener Kickoff Classic with West Virginia, Veland came off the bench, showcasing his hard-hitting style.

That late August afternoon, the Cornhusker defense shut out the Mountaineers 31-0. On Sept. 8, Nebraska faced Texas Tech in Lubbock, Tex. A similar fate befell his teammate, free safety Mike Minter. In the third quarter Minter tore the ACL in his left knee. Veland replaced Minter as the starter and finished the season with 26 tackles, including 13 unassisted, three pass interceptions and one pass breakup. Against the Red Raiders, Veland picked off a pass and returned it 35 yards.

His team, meanwhile, had lost starting quarterback Tommie Frazier to blood clots in his right leg. As the defense pulled together without Minter, the team rallied behind their new starting signal caller Brook Berringer.

"When we lost Tommie, that was a big thing. That was a big blow. I didn't know how we were going to react to that. But the defense knew that we had to pick it up and go to another level to achieve the goal that we had set. And that's what we did. And at the same time, the offense said, 'this isn't a one-man team.' We have a lot of players and one man is not going to make this team great. We are going to be great without that one man. And we just played above it. It wasn't like we changed a lot with our offense or our defense, because Brook was a very capable person of doing pretty much anything that Tommie had done. So we had all the confidence in the world in him. So we kept going all through the season. Brook led us through. We made it to that last game."

On Jan. 1, 1995, the Huskers returned to the Orange Bowl to face Miami for the national championship. In the home of the Hurricanes, Nebraska faced a boisterous unfriendly crowd, a capable quarterback and receiver corps, and a potent defense led by Lombardi Trophy winner Warren Sapp. The atmosphere within the Orange Bowl was hostile as Hurricane fans held an overwhelming majority in numbers. Less than a week before the matchup, the team attended an NFL playoff game featuring Miami and Kansas. Even within Joe Robbie Stadium, the fans were less than hospitable.

"We were wearing our Nebraska stuff and the fans were just rude. They were just up in our face saying this and that. 'You're terrible. You need to go back to Nebraska.'

"It just set up the whole event. It really did. They have some good fan support down there, I'll say that."

On game night, the players were not intimidated.

"It was loud and hostile. It was just crazy. But we just focused on what we came there to do. I mean, the crowd can't do anything to you but talk. We were there to do a job and went out there and did it, regardless of what the crowd said or did."

Miami took a ten-point lead into the second quarter, but a Brook Berringer 19-yard touchdown pass to tight end Mark Gilman narrowed the score to 10-7 at intermission. Veland said coach Tom Osborne's locker room speech was inspiring.

"Tom Osborne sounded like a prophet when he said that we needed to play hard and that we were going to wear them out come the fourth quarter. And it just came true, like the Lord gave him a vision. And everything just came true, like the way that he said it. We thank God for that."

The Hurricanes struck quickly in the third period, scoring on a Frank Costa to Jonathan Harris 44-yard pass with 13:19 remaining in the quarter. Nebraska added two points on a Costa sack in the end zone to trail 17-9 going into the final quarter.

In the fourth period, Osborne reinstalled starter Tommie Frazier who directed Nebraska on their final two scoring drives en route to a 24-17 victory.

"Tommie came in there and led us like a champ, like the true winner that he is.

"It was a very tough game. It was probably the most exciting game that I have ever been in in my life. The game went back and forth with the lead changes. They were a very aggressive team, a very fast team. And our defense hadn't been challenged by a team like that the whole year. But we all stepped up and listened to what coach Osborne told us.

"We came and got the monkey off Coach Osborne's back and proved something to those Florida teams and gave something back to our state. It was indescribable. It was great. I enjoyed that more than [winning] the second one [national title over Florida].

"We were just in a lot better condition than Miami. We were a stronger team. I think they had taken a week or two off before the bowl game. We only took a couple days off for finals. I don't think they were used to the style of football that we play–four quarters of smash-mouth football. And consequently, by the time the fourth quarter came, they really didn't have anything left."

The Blackshirts remained focused during the game's final minutes following Nebraska fullback Cory Schlesinger's fourth quarter go-ahead touchdown. A year earlier on the same field, Florida State had orchestrated a 65-yard drive in less than one minute to take the lead for good. That same scenario did not happen again. The Husker defense recorded two straight sacks on second and third downs. On fourth and long, Costa fired deep and was intercepted by senior rover Kareem Moss in the game's closing minute.

"We knew they were going to pass. They weren't going to run. But we weren't going to change anything we had done all day. We were still going to put on pressure. I don't think anybody was going to count their team out. We were still playing as hard as we could possibly play. And I think the only time any of us let out a sigh of relief was when Kareem Moss intercepted the ball and we knew the game was over."

The Huskers reloaded for title No. 2 in 1995. En route to the Fiesta Bowl, the Husker offense topped the 1983 Scoring Explosion by averaging 52.4 points each game. Nebraska's domineering defense held opponents to 13.6 points per contest and finished the season ranked second against the run, fourth in scoring defense, and sacked opponents 32 times for minus 231 yards. The Blackshirts also picked off 20 interceptions and caused 23 fumbles. Veland, a senior defensive captain, recorded 38 tackles, including 22 solos. He also broke up two passes, intercepted one, caused one fumble and recovered two. Against Oklahoma he returned a fumble 57 yards for a touchdown midway through the third quarter.

Three Big Eight teams ranked in the top-ten proved to be little more than victims as one of the greatest college football teams ever assembled pillaged its way through the season. On October 21, No. 8 Kansas State fell in Lincoln 49-25. One week later in Boulder, the Huskers toppled seventh-rated Colorado 44-21. And on November 11, the Huskers stomped tenth-ranked Kansas 41-3 in Lawrence.

The January 2 Tostitos Fiesta Bowl was hyped as a dogfight with No. 1 Nebraska's bulldozing ground attack against the high-speed aerial assault of No. 2 Florida's Fun-n-Gun offense.

"We were still being counted out again because Florida was a passing team, and they had scored so many points on a lot of people. But we were very confident. Going into that game, we knew what we were capable of and we were prepared for anything that was going to happen. They couldn't pick up our blitz, pretty much during the whole game. We had a quarterback and some backs who refused to go down. And that pretty much got us through the game. By half time, the game was pretty much over, to be honest. It was pretty much a rout."

Indeed, at intermission, the Huskers led 35-10 en route to a 62-24 victory.

During Veland's two-year period as a starter at free safety the Husker defense held numerous great offensive players and teams at bay. Florida quarterback, and eventual 1996 Heisman Trophy winner, Danny Wuerffel was sacked seven times and intercepted three times as his potent offense was held to only 269 yards total offense in the Fiesta Bowl. All-American running back and eventual two-time 2,000 yard rusher Troy Davis of Iowa State was held to 121 yards on 28 carries during the '95 regular season. In 1994, Colorado's potent offensive trio [All-American receiver Michael Westbrook, Heisman Trophy winner Rashaan Salaam, and All-Big Eight quarterback Kordell Stewart] was held to a mere seven points in Lincoln.

"That just shows when you practice well, you play well," Veland explained of his team's defensive dominance. "Have faith in your coaches. They know what they are doing. We knew we had good athletes to go along with theirs. If we played our coverages and our responsibilities we knew there weren't too many things that were going to hurt us, regardless of their athletes."

Veland added that team unity was an enormous factor en route to winning two straight national titles.

"You don't want to be divided. To beat somebody is to beat them from within. As long as we were together, we would have no problem if we played as hard as we could for each other. I think our class realized that. And we're all out there for a common goal."

Off the field, Tony's thoughts never completely strayed away from God. The defensive captain saw something in his close friend, roverback Mike Minter, that he wanted. During Veland's senior season, the pair roomed together prior to games. They would often talk late into the night about Christianity.

"One day we started talking about religion a little bit. I had seen him meeting with Ron Brown and I asked him about it and it sparked the whole thing. We talked about the Lord. After coming to the Lord we kept each other accountable."

In February 1996, Veland said he met with another friend, Lincoln Fellowship of Christian Athletes representative Chris Bubak to pray to receive Jesus Christ as Savior.

Looking back upon those brief years at UNL, Veland expressed gratitude for the people he said God placed in his life to prompt him in making a spiritual change.

"I had a lot of good people around me. I think they were trying to tell me something. I don't think all of the coaches really know how much of an influence they had on me, like Ron Brown, who had a huge influence on me because his faith is so strong. And coach Osborne, just the way that he carries himself and he always looks to the Lord first and he sticks up for his players. That had a huge impact on me then. There was Chris Bubak, who passed out cards at a team meeting that asked if we would be interested in a Bible study. He has been very instrumental in helping me. He and Diane Yeutter were probably the most important people.

"It was like the Lord was tapping me on my shoulder, telling me, 'Look, I'm trying to reach you. I've put all these people around you, so that you will turn to me. Why don't you go ahead and do it?' And one day I realized that I needed to turn my life over to the Lord and that happened in February 1996."

Following his conversion, Veland met often with Bubak for Bible study and to grow in his newfound faith. In 1996, the Denver Broncos sixth-round draft pick returned to the gridiron. There he served as a scout team player. Entering the '97 season, he improved to second team free safety. And as the developmental process within the NFL has not been without its growing pains, so has his faith faced similar challenges. Veland shared his greatest lessons in spiritual maturity.

"I'm not in control of my life, so I don't need to try to be. Because I can't do it. I can't beat sin—it's impossible without the help of the Lord. And you can't make it through this life without the Lord because there are going to be so many obstacles you will go through. There will be times when friends or family won't be able to comfort you or carry you through that situation. The only one who will be able to carry you will be the Lord."

And the peace he said he discovered has been through knowing his life is in God's hands.

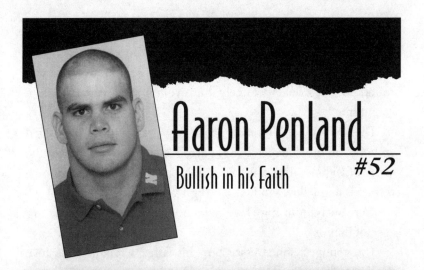

Aaron Penland

Bullish in his Faith

#52

**Backup inside linebacker,
four-year letterman 1992-95**

The youngest of four brothers, Aaron Penland grew up near downtown Jacksonville, Florida with a bull, three cows and a pair of horses in his backyard.

Penland, a 6-foot-1, 220-pound backup inside linebacker from the Husker's 1994-95 national championship teams, wore a peaceful, lazy smile when he thought of home.

"It's about four acres," he described the family spread in a thick southern drawl. "It's kind of funny. It's not downtown Jacksonville, but you can see the big tall buildings from where we're at."

Bonded in a strong Christian family rich with memories, Aaron recounted when his eldest sibling raised a bull calf.

"David Junior, he's kind of crazy. He got a calf and we raised it from a bottle.

"So, we had this 1800-pound Brahma bull in our backyard. We built a chute and David Junior rode him in the yard. That's how he got into bull riding. He competed for about three years."

The exhilaration of an eight second ride on the colossal "Willy Bully" never quite grabbed Aaron, however.

"I'm not that dumb," Penland smiled. "You could pet it and everything. You could sit up on his back and get him to chase you around. But it could definitely hurt you if you weren't careful around him."

The free-spirited monster-sized pet has, perhaps, remained symbolic of the independent Penland clan. Aaron's father, the owner of Cypress Trucking Lines in Jacksonville, has been known by friends and fellow workers as "Big Dave."

"Stay away from Big Dave's wrath!" Aaron warned with a dry sense of humor.

The youngest son stressed how his father served as a positive Christian role model throughout his life.

"Growing up I knew not to mess up or he was going to hold me accountable. He's a man of integrity. What he says is what he means. What he says usually happens. Everybody respects him. He comes through with his word. And he's going to keep you on track with your responsibilities and make you do them," Aaron grinned.

"I grew up in a Christian home. I went to church regularly, every time the door was open. I trusted Christ early on, around second grade. My parents raised me to have good moral standards."

And in building upon those family values, Aaron expressed that he has sought to save his virginity and thus better his future marriage.

"People ask why I am a virgin and I just tell them I'm a Christian. That's just something you are supposed to save until you're married. A lot of them laugh, but then they eventually come to respect me.

"I went to some charity senior basketball games this year and they started talking about girls and this subject came up that I was a virgin. And some of them said that if they had to do it over again that they would remain a virgin.

"I have had a girlfriend for three years now and it's getting more and more difficult. There's times when things can get out of hand in a hurry if you don't watch yourself. You don't know who you are going to marry. If you are dating a girl, you need to respect her. You might think you are going to end up with her. But if you take that girl's virginity, you can spoil it for her.

"God has the perfect mate out there for you. And if you just wait in His time, he will make it come about."

Penland stressed the potential for contracting sexually transmitted diseases should be a strong reason in itself to remain abstinate.

"There's no telling what you can get. A lot of these guys are just loading a gun and putting it to their head. Sometimes they don't even know the person they sleep with and there's no telling what they've got. How is that going to impact you 10 years down the road when you find that you've got something?"

Aaron added that he once had doubts about his personal relationship with God. Questions persisted during his senior year at University Christian High School if he was truly a Christian and would he spend eternity in heaven?

Those quandaries mounted during a school chapel service. He knew, to others he might not have been noticeably living in sin, but he recognized he was not committed to honoring God in all areas of his life. He went forward during an altar call, hoping to find some answers and if he could have assurance of eternal life.

"When the preacher spoke it really convicted me. I could really see that I wasn't living the way that Christ would have me to live. I just felt God's conviction that I needed to turn around and get things straight. I couldn't do anything about it without Christ.

"I started reading the Bible more and doing a daily Bible study. I believe I was saved in the second grade. But when I was a senior, the commitment really became real to me. I really understood what it meant. It was only through what He did on the cross that I could be saved and have eternal life. I just felt a peace that a big weight had been lifted off my shoulder and that I could have assurance that I was saved. I could know that I have eternal life and not question it."

The need for peace with God was evidenced on April 18, 1996 with the tragic death of a teammate, quarterback Brook Berringer. The 22-year Goodland, Kan. native passed away when the plane he was piloting crashed in a field near Raymond, Neb.

But Berringer was prepared for eternity after accepting Christ as Savior and Lord nearly eight months earlier. It was through the tutoring and prayers of Art Lindsay, a concerned gentleman in his early '60s, who had befriended Brook just a short time earlier.

"That was really sad," Aaron recalled. "I was just in shock. One minute Brook is there and at the end of the day he's gone. I was fixing to speak [at a Fellowship of Christian Athletes state gathering] and he was supposed to be there. It really hit me that life is short and you don't know when you are going to go. So you better be ready and be living your life for Christ.

"It's great how Christ uses people to reach the lost. I don't know if Art knew what he was getting into. And you don't know the impact that your life has on those around you. God might be using you for a specific person; to get them saved. And if you don't do your job, then beware that you might be their only hope of salvation. I think Brook's life and death has had a big impact on other players on the team. Because coach Osborne, Ron Brown, and Art Lindsay all talked about having eternal life through Christ and that Brook knew where he was going. I know that it had an impact on me to be a better witness in everything I do."

Aaron came to the Lincoln campus in 1991 as a walk-on after giving up a scholarship at Liberty University in Virginia. His burning desire was to play for a top football program with his brother Matt. During Aaron's redshirt freshman year in 1992, the pair played in three games, though they were not on the field at the same time.

Matt saw his final action that same season when he tore his ACL against Arizona State. Interestingly, the duo both played inside linebacker and would wear the number 52 during their careers. Following Matt's career-ending injury, his brother wore this number the next game.

Aaron spent his remaining years as a backup. And it was admittedly frustrating for the former Florida prep All-Stater.

"It's real aggravating because sometimes you don't get to play as much as you want at a great football school like Nebraska. Every guy that plays at Nebraska is a very competitive athlete, so it's difficult to sit on the bench when you're just as competitive as the next guy."

"So I called up Matt. And I was really mad.

"He asked me, 'Who are you playing for? Are you playing for God or are you playing for yourself? God is in control of everything.'"

The youngest brother then concluded, "Nothing happens to me that hasn't crossed God's desk. If He is ultimately in control of everything and if I am doing my best and playing my hardest, then there's nothing that I can do but put it in His hands. And am I playing for my glory or am I playing for God's glory? So it really doesn't matter if I'm the low man on the totem pole. I should be giving my best wherever I am at. If I'm on first team or on scout team, I'll give it my best because I'm playing for God and not myself.

"All in all, I think I put it in perspective. In the times of eternity, nobody is going to care who was the No. 1 guy. It's just fun while you're the able to play football. So have fun at it and contribute where you can. There's so many good players out there. There's big-time competition and it's tough."

Since his freshman scout team days, Colossians 3:23 has remained a favorite verse and a focal point in his life: "Whatever you do, work at it with all your heart, as working for the Lord, not for men." (NIV)

"I would try to go wide-open all the time," he recalled. "And some of the older guys would say, 'Why do you go so hard all the time? How do you find all this energy?'

"I have to give God the credit for letting me play with intensity."

Clester Johnson

A Cheerful Grin

#33

**All-Big Eight
Honorable-Mention wingback 1995,
three-year letterman 1993-95**

As a small child he probably wore his same ready grin. The youngest of three then mischievous brothers, Clester Johnson and his siblings wandered the streets of their gang-infested Pasadena suburb any time of day or night. The trio often stole candy or small items from grocery stores, he said. Various times following a theft the boy was pursued afoot, though he was never caught.

But those days of aimlessly traversing the concrete avenues of southern California disappeared forever with the murder of his single mother. In 1978, when Clester was five years old, a jealous boyfriend took the life of Vernetta Johnson, leaving the three brothers orphaned, he said. Despite the tragedy, Clester explained that good truly came following that horrible incident.

"My brother and I came to the conclusion that it was meant to happen, because it guided us to another place. We were living in the Los Angeles area at the time and she was a single mother with three boys. There was no telling what would have happened to us—gang life or whatever? It could have easily been a bad situation, but the death of my mother changed it all.

"While it wasn't easy, God used that experience to teach me some important things in life."

With the two elder boys living with different relatives, Vernetta's mother, Maxine Johnson, accepted young Clester into her Memphis, Tennessee home. There she nurtured the child with a love that would imprint his life forever. With his grandmother's God-fearing example, Clester grew up an optimist notwithstanding those harsh circumstances surrounding his early life.

Maxine Johnson was a short, stocky woman—deep in her faith and great in character. As the mother of eight grown children of her own, she provided young Clester with structure and loving discipline. In her home, the boy learned responsibility and self-reliance.

"My grandmother was very involved in the church. I respected her 100 percent. She was a very good Christian role model. She made me straighten up a lot. She would not allow me to hang out at night—period! She did what she had to do to make me see the light, so to speak, not only spiritually but just raising me as a young man. I had to wash dishes every night, because we didn't have a dish washer. I had to take out the trash and make my bed. I remember the first time I made my bed. She told me to take it apart.

"'That thing looks like a broke-back elephant', she used to say.

"So I had to start over and do it again."

The young boy found himself sitting beside his grandmother in church each week. And though he regularly sought distraction during the pastor's sermons, Clester said those words from the pulpit and his grandmother's example later impacted his life.

"At the time, I saw that as a burden though I knew it was important. I respected everything my grandmother taught me, but I was just being stubborn as a young man.

"I was real hyper as a little boy. My attention span wasn't very long. I can remember trying to listen to the preacher once or twice, but other than that, it was snickering, giggling, drawing pictures or

that type of thing. I used to wiggle my ears to try to make people laugh.

"Though I didn't really understand that structure in my life, going to church and stuff was important. I knew it was important to go to church and worship God."

In spite of his grandmother's positive molding upon his life, the youth found himself on the fringes of a bad crowd. Gang fights were prevalent within his neighborhood during his early teen years.

"I remember in eighth grade it would have been easy for me to join a gang. It was a rough neighborhood in north Memphis. I was around a lot of gang influence and had friends that did drugs. Those guys seemed cool. I looked up to them. It seemed the thing to do. I was real close to joining, but I didn't do it. I didn't want to get in trouble with my grandmother. And after awhile I knew that it was something that I didn't want to be a part of."

The following school year, Clester moved to the midwest and

away from his jungle-like neighborhood. A short visit to his relatives in Bellevue, Neb. whetted his desires for change. In that air force town he felt he would be able to attend a better school and have the opportunity to participate in better youth activities. Ultimately, he said the gang unrest in his neighborhood did not affect his decision.

"I didn't like going to school there. And when I came to Bellevue to visit and saw all the activities for youth, that made me want to go there."

In Bellevue he lived with his late mother's younger sister and her husband, Ellen and Ontee Biggs. Clester's needs for family, stability, and structure were again met in their home.

Clester and their son, his first cousin Ontee "Tojo" Biggs III, played football at Bellevue West High School together. In that community adjacent to southeast Omaha, Clester found his niche in athletics.

Johnson became an all-state quarterback for the Thunderbirds. He amassed 3,757 yards through the air, 712 on the ground, and scored 36 touchdowns in three years. Clester was also a teammate of fellow prep all-stater, future NU basketball standout and NBA point guard Eric Strickland.

The 5-foot-11-inch athlete also found success on the oval track and the wrestling mat. As a senior, Clester won the all-class gold medal in the 300-meter hurdles in state track. In only his second wrestling season, Clester said he lost a 1-0 decision in the Class A 189-pound state finals. Johnson and opponent Jon Adkisson of Columbus entered the match undefeated.

"It was one of the featured matches of the state tournament. It was a real tug of war out there. No one wanted to make a mistake."

With the loss, Johnson finished his senior wrestling season at 33-1 as his opponent improved to 34-0.

And for his athletic accomplishments, Clester Johnson was

named the *Omaha World-Herald* and *Lincoln Journal-Star* 1991 Nebraska Prep Athlete of the Year.

During that successful senior year, Clester moved in with his middle brother Sylvo as his Uncle Ontee and family were restationed in Korea with his duties in the Air force. During that period he accepted a scholarship to play football for the Nebraska Cornhuskers.

As a UNL frosh, the state's top prep athlete quickly found he would have to compete for playing time among some of the nation's best college football players. The Bellevue West graduate alternated to three different positions before finding his role as a receiver. As a redshirting freshman in 1991, he practiced at quarterback. He switched to cornerback the ensuing fall and eventually moved to wingback that same season. In 1994 as a junior, he briefly split practice time as a third-team quarterback behind Matt Turman when starter Brook Berringer was ailing from a punctured lung. A fifth-year senior in 1995, he at last earned a starting role at wingback. And the building process over those seasons was well worth it, he indicated.

As a freshmen, his 1991 recruiting class arrived in Lincoln with a vision for greatness. The passion of winning two national championships spread readily among his young teammates.

"I plainly remember us talking about it. All the freshmen used to have study hall together. And the one who talked about it the most was probably [outside linebacker] Dwayne Harris. He was really vocal. Other people included myself, [center] Aaron Graham, [inside linebackers] Phil Ellis and Doug Colman, [quarterback] Brook [Berringer], [split end] Reggie Baul, [free safety] Tony Veland, [offensive guard] Steve Ott, and [fullback] Jeff Makovicka.

"The reason I came to Nebraska was that I wanted to turn it around. When I first got here, there wasn't much unity on the football team. The year before [1990] they got plastered by [unranked]

Oklahoma 45-10 and then they got beat by [eventual United Press International National Champion] Georgia Tech [45-21 in the Citrus Bowl]. I was thinking maybe I could go down there and make the difference.

"I think that everyone that came in thought the same thing. We wanted to win the bowl games. We got tired of hearing that we couldn't win the big one. You hear that all the time and it makes you want to work harder. In the [Jan. 1, 1993 Orange Bowl] Florida State game where we lost by two touchdowns [27-14], I think that game was the key. Because in that game there were two plays how they beat us. We fumbled the ball on the 2-yard line and they got an easy touchdown off that and then there was one more play like that. And other than that, it was a 14-14 game.

"That next year Florida State was the best team in the country. And we were undefeated and were a 17-point underdog."

A backup behind junior Abdul Muhammad, Johnson finished the Jan. 1, 1994 Orange Bowl game with three receptions for 30 yards. His biggest highlight came with 5:59 remaining in the second quarter. Quarterback Tommie Frazier fired a bullet that a tightly covered Johnson tipped into the hands of teammate Reggie Baul who scored a 34-yard touchdown. The score gave Nebraska new life and a 7-3 lead. But in the end, his team came up short by two points. Nebraska's missed 45-yard field goal at the gun capped a dogfight in which the underrated Huskers had outplayed the mighty Seminoles. Despite the near miss at a national title, Cornhuskers players held their heads high. They left the field united in purpose to win the national title the following season.

"I think the more unified we got, the better the team got. Coach Osborne implemented a unity council and discussed how we talked to each other. He also talked about what we do off the field that distracts us from doing better on the field. We needed to encourage each other more and keep each other out of difficult situations. So, collectively we had more guys wanting to move in a better direction."

And with the team's unity of spirit and focus, combined with high-caliber athletic talent, Nebraska returned to the Orange Bowl on Jan. 1, 1995 for another shot at the elusive national crown. The No. 1 and undefeated Cornhuskers faced a familiar rival they had never beaten in Tom Osborne's head coaching tenure, third-ranked Miami.

"We came down there focused," recalls Clester. "We knew that we could do it. We made some mistakes in that game that made it closer than it probably should have been. We had to overcome the fact that it was in Miami. If that game had been in Lincoln, I guarantee that it wouldn't have been close."

A 14-yard touchdown run by fullback Cory Schlesinger with 2:46 remaining sealed Nebraska's 24-17 victory.

"That was a great memory. In the locker room we were jumping around. It was a mad house in there. I couldn't believe it."

As a fifth-year senior, Clester started nine games during the 1995 national championship season. Typically displaying his 33.5-inch vertical jump pass catching ability in a game, Johnson recorded 22 receptions for 367 yards and scored two touchdowns.

On Oct. 28 at seventh-ranked Colorado, Johnson caught three passes for 72 yards, including a high-jumping 52-yard touchdown reception. The score put NU up 21-7 late in the first quarter en route to a 44-21 victory.

"We had put in this new play in practice. I was looking forward to it in the game. Colorado had a pretty aggressive defense. With the type of formation we were in, they were going to be thinking run. So when I came out of the backfield, everything happened as planned except that [quarterback] Tommie [Frazier] under threw it a little bit. But I had a better jump on the ball and I went up and got it. The defender lost where I was and fell down. I still had my balance, so I turned around and took off."

The decisive win in Boulder vaulted Nebraska from No. 2 into the top spot.

On Jan. 2, 1996, Nebraska pasted then No. 2 and undefeated Florida 62-24 at the Fiesta Bowl in Tempe, Ariz. With the victory, the Huskers closed out a 12-0 season without a close game. Against the Gators, Johnson led Nebraska receivers with two catches for 43 yards. The senior also recorded one unassisted tackle.

"We won convincingly. That was the most dominating team in college football history. There were no close games. And I was on that team."

The football memories were truly great. However, in spite of the accolades and his cheerful disposition, Clester was admittedly searching for purpose. The party scene ultimately left him empty and feeling guilty, he said.

"I went to all the clubs. Now I don't miss it at all. I think that is partly maturity. I knew in the first place that it wasn't right. I knew that being with all these girls wasn't right. I knew that drinking and partying wasn't right. But the peer pressure influenced my choices."

Clester found himself searching for God. The Christian influence of his grandmother had continually been felt since he was a child. Yet he saw Christianity merely as an upright and moral teaching that could serve as a good luck charm. He attended football game day chapels in hopes that it would enhance his team's on-field success.

"Every time I went to chapel, we won, it was good luck."

He said the hypocrisy of some so-called church leaders turned him off to Christianity.

"Seeing spiritual leaders like the Jim Bakkers and the Jimmy Swaggarts get in trouble was a turn off. But I had to understand that people weren't perfect. And just because these people were doing wrong, that didn't mean that worshipping God was not right."

A person's actions often tend to speak louder than their words.

And just as a young Clester respected his grandmother for living what she preached, Johnson found positive role models within the ranks of his football coaches.

"Coach Osborne and coach Brown, those two were examples. The way they lived their lives, they really seemed happy, even though they might be down, they had something to fall back on. Those two guys had Someone that was always there for them."

The impressionable wingback talked occasionally with his position coach, Ron Brown, about Christianity and Islam, and religion in general.

"I questioned coach Brown about different religions. I was contemplating, 'Should I dedicate my life to this?'

"I was sure I would dedicate my life to Christ some day, but I continued to put off the decision. But when [former Nebraska quarterback] Brook [Berringer] died [in a plane crash April 18, 1996] I decided I had better do it now. Because you don't know about tomorrow. And so, that just brought it all together.

"At the funeral a lot of people spoke on Brook's behalf and they talked about how he committed himself to Christ. And that if they hadn't accepted Christ, they should do it at the funeral. Coach Brown put it in terms of football. 'Jesus Christ is throwing a pass to you. Are you going to drop it this time or are you going to catch it?' It didn't take long for me to realize that I wanted to make that catch."

Two days following Berringer's funeral in Goodland, Kansas, Clester met with Lincoln Fellowship of Christian Athletes representative Chris Bubak to pray to receive Christ as Savior. Johnson wanted the new life he said he saw in Berringer.

"When he died, he went to heaven. I saw that Brook was happy. When he wasn't playing [behind starter Tommie Frazier], he did not complain whatsoever. He didn't make a fuss about it and people didn't even realize it. How many guys can say that they wouldn't complain about it? Obviously he was content.

"My sense of urgency was to commit myself and not put it on the back burner. I learned that you have to be born spiritually. Which I did on the 23rd of April."

And with that decision, the cheerful grin Clester had worn throughout life became an outward expression of his newfound faith and purpose.

"It's very important to have Jesus Christ in your life. Not only when the roads are bad, but when the roads in your life are good you need Him."

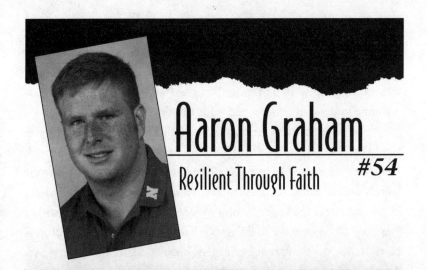

Aaron Graham

Resilient Through Faith
#54

**All-American center 1995, All-Big Eight 1994-95,
1995 NCAA Today's Top Eight Award winner,
Academic All-American 1995,
Academic All-Big Eight 1993-95,
1995 NU offensive captain,
four-year letterman 1992-95**

The most hostile battles in football are often fought on the front lines. And for former All-American center Aaron Graham of Nebraska's 1994-95 national championship teams, those intense on-field collisions have proven to be character revealing.

"Sometimes it's rough," said the 6-foot-4 285-pound lineman. "But I draw a symbol of the cross on my wrist tape and that gives me a chance before every play to look down at the hand that I snap the ball with and really remind myself who I'm playing for out on that field. It really helps me to stay focused in times where I might let my mouth slip. It keeps me focused on who I'm playing for."

That concentration has reflected his perseverance through the difficult struggles of life. And those pen markings of the cross have borne an urgent message following the tragic death of his close friend and late college teammate, quarterback Brook Berringer.

"It's really been evident to me that championships only mean so much," Graham stated. "And I think with Brook died, I lost some interest in all that. Even though it's great and we had an outstanding time and we accomplished a lot of things.

"The big picture is serving God. I think we were able to serve God the way He wanted us to, to be champions out on the field. But that's done and over. God doesn't want us to sit back on our laurels and watch time pass by. He wants us to be active and sharing. I really feel the urgency now. We're not guaranteed tomorrow. We need to be sure we're living our lives the way that God intended us to live it. I think that because of Brook's death, that's been evident to me now more than ever."

The passing of his late friend was not the first time he has lost someone close. In May 1991, his mother passed away due to complications from leukemia.

It was December 1990 during his senior year in high school in Denton, Texas when she was diagnosed. And in mid-March, only weeks after he signed his letter of intent to Nebraska, she would undergo a bone marrow transplant.

"They gave her a 60 percent chance for survival, but she didn't make it. Ironically, the person next to her had less chance to survive, but did survive. On May 3, a month and a half later, she passed away due to complications. "Naturally, that was one of the toughest things I've ever had to go through. It's something that you can never prepare for no matter how ready you think you are. People who haven't lost a relative or parent or somebody who is really close to them can't understand what it's like until it happens to them. It's really hard. I had never lost anybody else who was as close to me. So, naturally, having your mom pass away is pretty difficult."

Aaron coped with the death by relying on his faith, he said.

"It was through my faith in God and just a lot of prayer; a lot of help with my friends and people in my church."

Jay Garner, a tight companion since junior high, was there to understand and provide support.

"One of my best friends back in Texas had his father pass away when he was 12 years old. And it was kind of weird that he ended up being there for me when I'm 17 years old and my mom passed away. He helped a lot.

"I moved to Denton when I was in seventh grade and his dad passed away a year previous to that from a stroke. We just became real close friends from seventh grade on through high school. "We were so much alike and so much like brothers. It's not something that's necessarily a positive, but to have where both of us have lost a parent, you can definitely relate to each other a lot easier.

"I remember always trying to think about putting myself in his place and how he would react to certain situations. And know how he would react to situations when people would ask what his dad does for a living or something like that. And, ironically, five years later, I was having to deal with those same questions. And maybe with having him there, it made it a lot easier."

During that period, Aaron and his immediate family drew closer as well. But only a short time later they would be separated as his father remained in Denton, his sister returned to school at Texas Tech, and Aaron moved to Lincoln.

"My sister was at college and I left for Nebraska a month later. I left for Nebraska on June 5. It was a decision where I told my dad that I would stick around as long as he wanted me to. And he told me, 'No, we're just going to keep on going and not change any plans we have made.'

"And it was kind of hard because it was a time right afterwards where we were real close and were all leaning on each other and the next thing you know we all had to turn and go our separate ways. So, it was pretty difficult there for a while.

"Definitely, the deepest spiritual growth I've had was after my mom passed away. I still believe the closest that I have ever been to God is that summer afterwards. I came up to Lincoln and really did a lot of searching and trying to find some answers to a lot of questions that I had. And, not being around your immediate family and the church you grew up in, it was a little bit more difficult. But I think I found the answers that I was looking for and it helped me to have a better understanding."

As a senior at Nebraska, the soft-spoken team captain sought to encourage hurting youth in the community. He served as a speaker for Charlie Brown's kids, an organization that ministers to area youth who have suffered the loss of a parent.

"I sit down and give them my story and what happened to me. And I just give them some ideas and some pointers to what helped me get through the situation. If that would have happened to me when I was younger, I would have hoped that there would have been somebody out there to help me and come and talk to me about it who would understand."

Aaron's challenges within the confining measurements of the gridiron have been incredibly small compared to those hardships.

But through those on-field adversities, his perseverance proved as strong.

On Nov. 25, 1994, No. 1 Nebraska faced Oklahoma in Norman with passage rights to the Orange Bowl and national championship at stake. But Graham was battling a micro-sized foe—the flu virus.

"I had the flu for three days prior to the Oklahoma game. The first half was pretty much just a blur. I was dizzy. I just felt terrible."

Trainers attached a respirator to him to attempt to slow down his breathing, he said. Still feeling the effects of the illness, he followed the team onto the field for the second half.

"I felt faint, dizzy, and everything. I just couldn't believe that this was happening to me. I just couldn't imagine having to sit out the second half of this game, especially for a sickness and not an injury. I really appreciate [receivers] coach [Ron] Brown. He turned to me and he could see the frustration and the pain in my eyes and he said, 'Ask the Lord to give you strength.'

"So I went over and knelt down by the bench and I just simply asked God to give me strength to make it through the second half. And the honest truth was that I opened my eyes up from that prayer and my focus became clear. My breathing slowed down and I played the entire second half of that game. It was gone, as far as being sick for that day. It was truly a moving experience for me."

Graham rates among Nebraska's best centers ever. He paved openings as a three-year starting member of a Cornhusker offensive line that produced two other All-Americans during its 1994-95 national championship seasons. Graham and company played nearly flawless football. The 1995 front wall never allowed a single sack and was flagged for only six penalties en route to the school's 12th NCAA rushing title. In '94, the Nebraska "Pipeline" gave up only six sacks, was called for holding four times, and burned a path for ball carriers to average 340 yards on the ground.

Graham and the rest of the team displayed an intense unity and focus to win every game. The interior lineman played in three consecutive national championship games, including Nebraska's 1994–95 back-to-back title matches. Nebraska's only loss during that three-year 36-1 run was an 18-16 loss to eventual National Champion Florida State in the January 1, 1994 Orange Bowl. The Cornhuskers' 45-yard field goal attempt sailed wide left on the game's final play.

Following that heart-breaking loss, the squad adopted the slogan "Unfinished Business" in their quest to return to and win the big game. During the 1994 sultry August two-a-days, Nebraska's Memorial Stadium scoreboard flashed "1:16" as a reminder of the game time remaining when the Huskers last held the lead against Florida State. That mental image spurned players in the weight room, throughout practices, and during each game.

"There was nothing but determination the entire next year to get back to the Orange Bowl and get another chance at it and win the thing this time. And we did. It was character building in that you never give up, you keep on going, and learn from your mistakes."

In 1995, it was business as usual as the Nebraska offense pounded opponents to average 52.4 points a game en route to a 62-24 drumming of No. 2 Florida in the National Championship Fiesta Bowl at Tempe, Ariz.

The offensive lineman returned to the land of the desert sun as a 1996 fourth-round draft pick by the Arizona Cardinals. That fall he started nine games as a rookie. He entered the '97 season as the No. 2 center. Focused, Graham carries those disciplines called hope and perseverance through the professional level and throughout life.

Brook Berringer
Hope amidst Adversity
#18

Second Team All-Big Eight Quarterback 1994,
Academic All-Big Eight 1995,
four year letterman 1992-95

"If you had somebody you wanted your son to be like, Brook would be a good place to start," Nebraska coach Tom Osborne stated only short hours following former quarterback Brook Berringer's tragic death in a plane crash. "He was one of those guys who stood for all the right things. I was very close to Brook, personally. Brook was a great guy. He deserves to be remembered."

On Thursday, April 18, 1996, 22-year old Berringer and his passenger Tobey Lake, brother of his girlfriend, took off in a 1946 Piper Cub from a small private rural airstrip in Raymond, Neb. at approximately 2:30 pm for what was to have been a brief ride. The plane reportedly ascended to approximately 250 feet, stalled, fell into a nose-dive and crashed in a field.

Brook's death happened the same day he was to join a handful of teammates and coaches in speaking at the state Fellowship of Christian Athletes banquet in Lincoln. The tragedy also preceded the National Football League draft by two days. Berringer would likely have found opportunity in the NFL. Some analysts ranked him among the top five quarterbacks available.

During the majority of his Cornhusker career, Berringer spent his time as a backup to the 1995 All-American signal caller, Tommie Frazier.

But when Frazier was sidelined during the '94 championship run with a blood clot located behind his right knee, Berringer started and won seven games. He passed for 1,295 yards on 94 of 151 attempts. In 1995 the Goodland, Kan. native had to return to his role as a backup. During the regular season he threw for 252 yards on 26-of-51 attempts with no interceptions or touchdowns. His four-year career statistics included 1,769 yards through the air, 396 yards on the ground, and 20 touchdowns.

Though Berringer possessed the ability to start almost anywhere else in the country, he never publicly complained about it. He was a team player.

"He handled a tough situation as well and with about as much dignity as anybody ever could, in terms of his playing situation," said coach Osborne.

Berringer started for the first time on Oct. 1, 1994 against Wyoming after Frazier was sidelined with a blood clot behind his right knee. Berringer played the game's second half with a partially collapsed lung and several cracked ribs. He suffered the injury from a hit during NU's final first half scoring drive. That scoring series was symbolic of Berringer's ability to persevere through adversity. His team trailed 21-7 with 2:12 remaining in the half. The six-four native of Goodland, Kan. completed seven straight passes for 59 yards and rushed for a gritty five-yard touchdown. And despite the injury, he directed Nebraska back from a 21-14 halftime deficit, rushing for a total of 74 yards, scoring three TDs and going 15-of-22 through the air for 131 yards.

Berringer started the following week against Oklahoma State, suiting up with a protective flak jacket and his lung reinflated. He did not play the final two quarters as halftime X-rays showed the

lung was again deflating after taking another hit.

His lung and sore ribs still ailing him, Brook did not start Oct. 15 in Manhattan against his home-state Kansas State Wildcats. But the gamer came in for the first half's final series as Nebraska held a 7-6 lead established by sophomore walk-on quarterback Matt Turman. Berringer played the remainder of the game en route to a 17-6 win.

Next week at Missouri, though his game remained limited as he continued to heal, Berringer threw for 152 yards and three touchdowns.

On October 29, a day marked as Nebraska's 200th consecutive home sellout, Berringer did not disappoint against second-ranked Colorado. With his physical condition improved, the junior quarterback showcased his best performance.

Coming into the matchup that would likely set the stage for the national championship, the Nebraska offense needed to outplay Colorado's most explosive corps ever. Run-pass specialist Kordell Stewart, a second-team All-American quarterback, directed the attack with first-team All-Americans Michael Westbrook at wide receiver and Rashaan Salaam at running back. The Buffalos were flying high following a Sept. 24th 27-26 come-from-behind road victory over fourth-ranked Michigan. Highlighting the game was "the catch"–a 64-yard Stewart-to-Westbrook Hail Mary reception at the gun.

But Berringer was not intimidated by his opposing counterpart's past glory. The tall Husker quarterback completed 12-of-17 passes for 142 yards and one touchdown. With 10:42 remaining in the third, Berringer lofted a 30-yard touchdown pass to tight end Eric Alford to put the Huskers up 24-0. The 1994 Heisman trophy winner, Salaam, scored the Buffalo's lone touchdown as Nebraska vaulted from No. 3 to the top of the polls following the 24-7 victory.

Following that pivotal contest, the tall, dark-haired woodsman's words reflected a genuine, yet non-boasting, sense of confidence and leadership.

"I think we proved we're No. 1," he said calmly. "I think we're going to come out and continue to prove it all season. We knew we would come out and play well, even through adversity and when no one else was giving us much of a chance."

The Huskers solidified the No. 1 ranking the following week in Lincoln with a 45-17 win over Kansas. Berringer passed for 267 yards, hitting 13 of 18 with no interceptions and two touchdowns.

Brook finished the 1994 season with road wins over Iowa State and Oklahoma and directed Nebraska's passing attack during the Jan. 1, 1995 National Championship Orange Bowl against Miami. Tommie Frazier, recovered from the blood clots, started against the Hurricanes, but struggled through the first quarter. Berringer came off the bench, hitting 8-of-15 passes for 81 yards, including a 19-yard TD strike to tight end Mark Gilman midway through the second quarter.

But adversity would mount again for Berringer one minute into the fourth quarter. Trailing 17-9, the Cornhuskers appeared certain to turn the complexion of the game as they lined up at Miami's 4-yard line following a high snap to the punter that was kicked through the end zone.

The signal caller from Goodland rolled back to pass. Unable to find an open receiver he lofted it over the field, intending it to fall out of bounds incomplete. But defender Earl Little snagged it from the back of the end zone for a touchback. On Nebraska's next series, Osborne re-installed Frazier at the helm as they mounted their fourth quarter 24-17 comeback en route to winning the 1994 national championship.

Berringer's duties during the 1995 repeat title run were strictly as a backup to Frazier. That season he struggled with a ruptured bursa sac in his right knee, missing the Missouri and Kansas State games. He saw the most playing time in September against Michigan State and Pacific. On Jan. 2, during the national championship rout of No. 2 Florida in the Fiesta Bowl, Berringer scored on a 1-yard quarterback sneak with 4:44 remaining to put Nebraska up 62-18.

On the field, Brook Berringer displayed NFL potential during the 1994 championship run. As a backup to Heisman Trophy runner-up Frazier in '95, Berringer exemplified the proven character of a team player in accepting his role.

"At the time I couldn't put my finger on what was going on in Brook's life," reflected his close friend, All-American center Aaron Graham. "He came to practice every day. I never heard him complain. In the past, he would have been disappointed that he wasn't getting a shot. He had a different outlook on the whole situation. When his opportunities came, he came in and did his job."

"[During] my whole career I've been on both ends of the spectrum," the late Berringer said in an interview in December 1995, short days prior to the 1996 National Championship Fiesta Bowl in Tempe, Ariz. "I've enjoyed the starting position and I've had to suffer through the frustrations of not getting to play at all. But, you know, through this whole ordeal I have been able to use my faith as something that is just a complete comfort. And it just takes away a lot of those feelings."

Ironically, Berringer committed himself to that faith in Jesus Christ on August 24, 1995–the day Frazier was announced as the starting quarterback. The date bore even greater significance as it was the birthday of his late father, Warren, who died of cancer when Brook was only seven.

Brook's spiritual journey was ignited by the prayers of a financial advisor in his early '60s. Art Lindsay, a former pastor and missionary, acted on an inner conviction to minister to this young man from northwest Kansas.

"I remember so clearly the first time God ever told me to pray for Brook," Lindsay said at the FCA gathering following Berringer's fatal plane crash. "I was sitting in the south stadium and he entered the game. I had never heard his name before, but when I heard the name, I started praying for him then. And it intensified across the years to the point where I was praying for him every day, and finally we got together."

"Art Lindsay began communicating with me through some letters that [receivers] coach [Ron] Brown had given me of a prayer he was praying for me every day and it was inspiring," the late Berringer said. "And I hadn't even met the guy.

"Finally, I was able to meet with Art and we started meeting together and having some fellowship. And through him, together, I accepted the Lord as my Savior and it was an incredible thing. It was something that I have really thought a lot about through the last four years.

"Through college I had a lot of positive influence through coach Brown and coach Osborne. And it was something that was really weighing pretty heavily on my mind—and it was through Art and through the fellowship that we had. We sat down together and I just gave my life to the Lord and accepted Him as my Savior."

Brown recalled when the elder gentleman first approached him about passing those letters of spiritual insight along to the young quarterback.

"A guy like Art Lindsay sends me letters back in 1994 regarding Brook Berringer," Brown said. "Now, Art doesn't know Brook from a hole in the wall. But do you think it was coincidental that Art Lindsay just starting sending letters to Brook Berringer? I think what happened was that he [Art] was very available to God. I think he was very open. And God said, 'Art, I am doing a work in Brook Berringer's life and I want you to join me. Will you join me?'

"And I think Art was faithful in sending letters to me to give to Brook. I didn't know how Brook would respond. He was one of those guys, you know, who I didn't want to push. But [after reading them] he [Brook] would say, 'Oh no, I love them. Man, they're great.'

"And this was during Brook's string of consecutive big-time games when Frazier was injured his junior year. And Brook was very open to those letters."

Thus, late in the summer, after Art and Brook met together several times to talk about the Lord, the 22-year old finally made a decision. It was a resolution through prayer to accept Christ's death on the cross as the payment for his sins.

"It was an incredible thing," Berringer said. "It was something that was weighing heavy on my mind. And when I did it, I just felt a great relief. A lot of things were lifted off my shoulders when I did that."

And because of his faith in God, Brook said he found hope through whatever adversity he faced.

"When I have something more specific to focus on, like eternal life and my faith and Christianity, and my yearning just to grow in that faith—it brings everything, the whole scheme of things into focus. It's just amazing, the difference that it's made in my life. I know where I'm headed, the ultimate goal and it brings everything into perspective. And it makes football, although it is a big part of my life, something that is not as important as maybe I once thought. And it really prioritizes things in my life."

And that faith provides hope for eternity amidst his tragic passing.

A former teammate, Nebraska All-American center Aaron Graham, reflects on his friendship with the late Brook Berringer.

"Inspiration"

During his early seasons at Nebraska, quarterback Brook Berringer would never admit to his friends that he was pure country.

The 6-foot-4-inch freshman arrived on campus from rural northwest Kansas in a Mustang vibrating top-40 hits. An instinctive woodsman, the Goodland native breathed hunting.

Brook's love for the outdoors had been nurtured by his late father, Warren, when he was barely a toddler. During those early months of his childhood, his mother, Jan, would send the pair with lunch and diaper bag when they traversed the land for game. His passion for nature became an extension of himself as he grew into manhood. For Brook Berringer, to live was to scan the fields for quail or pheasant and breathe the crisp fall morning air.

While residing in Lincoln, Berringer walked several tree lines with his close friends, center Aaron Graham and linebacker Phil Ellis. A Texas native, Graham loved everything the great outdoors stood for, from country music to a Chevy truck. But the tall Kansan found his hunting companion's tastes simply offensive.

"I remember when we would go hunting we would always take my truck," recalled Graham in his friendly Texas drawl. "And I remember turning on the radio and he would say, 'Turn the station! We aren't listening to that stuff.'

"And he used to just let me have it for wearing Wranglers, ropers, and a cowboy hat and things like that."

Brook's fancies changed, however. He even learned to play the guitar and frequently strummed country tunes.

"I think he was so country that he tried to get away from it, almost as far as he could," Graham smiled. "Because Goodland, Kansas is about as country as you can get."

The tall woodsman was quiet, independent, and competitive, said Graham.

"We had a lot of the same interests. Earlier, in a lot of ways it kind of repelled us rather than brought us together. Brook has always had that competitive nature about him, and so did I. And when we would go out hunting together, it would almost turn into a contest instead of just getting out there and having fun."

The two would often haggle over deep issues, like which tree line to walk.

"I'm the type of person that gets along with just about everybody, but I probably had more arguments with Brook than with anybody I have ever had in my whole life," Graham shook his head with a grin.

In the huddle, the All-American center described Berringer as a confident, soft-spoken leader who was "tougher than nails." Berringer and roommate Phil Ellis would often taunt each other as friends on and off the field.

"Phil, without a doubt was probably the toughest guy on our team. People always thought [defensive tackle] Christian [Peter] was, but I think Phil was even more so.

"And sure enough, one night down in our basement they got to wrestling and Brook pinned Phil. And that was the end of that," Graham chuckled to himself. "And I would have never bet [on it]!"

Brook was unafraid of various challenges, whether it was fixing the head coach's attire or flying.

Tom Osborne left his office for his workout dressed in mid-calf length sweats and a straight-bill cap. He stepped onto the elevator with Berringer and Graham.

"Coach Osborne was always a little bit intimidating. He tried not to be, but he just was. And Brook didn't have that attitude toward him at all. Brook would just say whatever he wanted to."

Berringer simply shook his head at Osborne with a disapproving grin. The coach smiled back in wonder of what was wrong.

"And Brook reaches over and takes off his hat and rounds his bill for him like a 'V' and puts it back on his head. Then he bent down and pulled his sweats [from mid-calf] all the way down to his shoes. Coach Osborne was just shaking his head laughing at him. And he goes, 'There you go, coach.' And he patted him on the arm."

The outdoorsman typically had a dry wit about him.

"He had more one-liners than anybody I've ever met in my whole life," Graham mused.

"For example, we would be driving to go hunting and he'd wave and somebody wouldn't wave back. And he'd be like, 'Well if I knew your hand was broke I wouldn't have waved at you.'

"He gave people nicknames," the offensive lineman laughed. "He nicknamed [backup quarterback] Matt Turman, 'Turmanator.' People have used that all over. Well, Brook came up with that nickname. He had about 20 nicknames for me, like Fat Daddy Graham."

Brook also loved the exhilaration of flying.

"I flew with him probably three times or so. It was a thrill. We rented this plane. It didn't cost us very much to rent the plane for an hour. And that's as much fun as you can have. This plane was teeny-tiny. You couldn't have fit two bigger bodies in there. And we took off and were getting blown around and he was just in total control. He was a very good pilot.

"There are so many variables that you have to control when you are in a plane like that. And Brook's attitude was that he was ready to challenge those things. He was very safe. He didn't try anything crazy.

"We were just flying around and he said, 'Do you want to try a stall?'

"'What is that? That doesn't sound good.'

"So, he said, 'Well, I'll show you.'

"And what am I going to do, grab the wheel and say, 'no!'?

"And he pulls the stick back and we just start climbing vertically. And the object is that you climb to a point where the aircraft can't climb anymore. And you fall backwards and then you tilt out of it forward.

"And I was like, 'That's enough of that! We ain't doing any more stalls. It's about time that we go land,' Graham recounted with a laugh.

"So he was laughing because he knew he was in control. It wasn't a worry to him. But I found enough courage to go up a couple more times with him," Aaron smiled.

Never backing away from a challenge, the wearer of jersey No. 18 was a gamer. With Tommie Frazier sidelined for eight games with blood clots in 1994, Berringer came in and played in four games with a partially collapsed lung.

Initially injured Oct. 1 while playing Wyoming, Brook suited up the following week against Oklahoma State wearing a flak jacket with his lung re-inflated. Halftime X-rays revealed the lung had partially recollapsed, but Brook was not ready to quit playing until that diagnosis.

"I remember [wingback] Clester [Johnson] saying that he was standing right next to Brook and could just hear his lung when he was breathing.

"And Brook knew that his lung had recollapsed and they were going to take him in at half time. But he wasn't about to forfeit that opportunity. He was going to stay in there no matter what."

Berringer posted a 7-0 record that season, but lost the starting reins to Frazier at the Orange Bowl and for the remainder of his career. Though he had NFL potential and the ability to start at several other universities, he did not publicly complain. The All-American center notes that prior to Berringer's conversion, the tall quarterback might have privately shared feelings of disappointment. But during the 1995 season, Brook was at peace amidst his circumstances.

"I never heard him complain," stated Graham. "In the past it was a different story. He would have been more verbal with me, but never with other players or coaches. He would be disappointed, saying that he's not even getting a shot. But [in 1995] he came into the games [to substitute for an injured Tommie Frazier], like Michigan State, and did his job. He just had a whole different attitude. He just sat back waiting, being prepared if the same thing happened again."

Though Brook Berringer passed away in the prime of his life, with two national championships behind him and a pro football career before him, Aaron said that by accepting Christ he was prepared for eternity.

"Just to think that he made that decision at the right time, I think it demonstrates an urgency to everyone that we don't know when our time is coming. It brought me to tears just thinking about him. You have to thank [mentor] Art [Lindsay] for his witness. That made the difference in Brook's salvation. But it's been rough just because he was just such a good friend of mine. All the tears I have cried for him have not been tears of sadness, but tears of joy."

And despite the tragedy, positive fruit has abounded among his former teammates.

"Out of our senior class, I know that there's been several guys who have given their life over to the Lord just because of this. A lot of his friends have been coming to our Bible studies and are really searching, because they want what Brook had. He's made a tremendous impact."

Graham has frequently contemplated that need to make a positive impact with his life. That message has been captured in an illustration produced by the Fellowship of Christian Athletes. The picture depicted an FCA huddle of teenage boys and a young boy curiously looking in from the outside. The child stood in the foreground wearing a football jersey with the No. 18.

"I have that picture hanging up in my living room and I look at it all the time. The inscription underneath it says, 'Influence.'

"When you first look at that, the meaning is that this little boy is being inspired by these other guys. But it's a total reverse [symbolism] now because Brook is looking in and he is the inspiration for us."

And to us all.

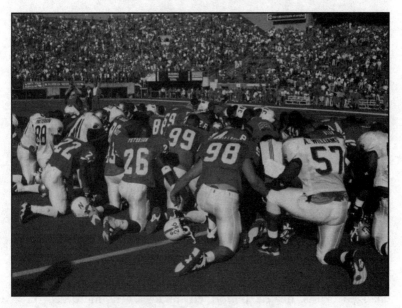

A Word from Coach Ron Brown

For a moment in time, Nebraskans knew what if felt like to be on top in the world of college football with our back-to-back national championships in the '90s. However, that pleasure, although perhaps forever etched in our hearts, eventually became dull for some and many began to crave for something that had greater meaning.

In 1979, at the end of my senior year at Brown University, I too began a search for something more satisfying than football championships. I wasn't a national champion or All-American. Yet my small world still defined me as successful. I was adopted from an inner city orphanage as a little child by two wonderful people, Arthur and Pearl Brown, who became my parents. Neither, because of family responsibilities, finished their high school education. Yet, with their inspiration, I was about to become an Ivy League graduate and sign a free agent contract with the Dallas Cowboys. Those in my world claimed I had overcome many obstacles to be this successful. Yet, deep down inside, the square pegs of academic, athletic, and social success weren't fitting in the round holes that could only be filled by the one who made me, God.

I had heard all my life about Jesus Christ. I believed intellectually and conceptually in Him, but I had no relationship with Him. I was living my life on my own, calling my own shots, making my own plans, pulling myself up the ladder of success by my own bootstraps until I came to an end of myself one day.

All of these things that I was chasing began to leave me high and dry with an emptiness inside. Some call it a weakness, a crutch. I thank God that I finally realized I was too weak to control life and make it revolve around Ron Brown. Every person, including myself, was too weak to totally fulfill me. I thank God for the "crutch" that He offered to me as a free gift—the cross of Jesus Christ.

Jesus as God in the flesh came down to earth, lived a sinless life, changed hearts, healed, performed miracles, was murdered on a cross for my sins, then was buried. That day in 1979, I finally faced myself to realize only Jesus could give me the love, purpose, and direction on earth, as well as the home in heaven that I wanted so badly. It was then I banked my life by faith that Jesus rose out of that grave, back to heaven and is coming back one day to rule forever. That day I asked Jesus Christ into my heart. I decided to repent and turn from my sinful life. Jesus will enter and rule the life of anyone who believes and trusts in Him as Savior and Lord for forgiveness of their sins. That day was the greatest day of my life. It was the day I joined God's team.

I'm not always a great player for Him. I fail Him many times. But I am a team member for life and eternity. Jesus is my coach forever. Is He yours?

Accepting Christ can be illustrated by a football analogy of catching a pass. Coaching receivers for the last ten years, I've come to the basic conclusion that even good players at times drop passes for three reasons:

First, the ball is coming. And when it gets about six inches away from their hands they begin to think about turning upfield, juking defenders, crossing the goal line, becoming heroes. They then begin to look at the goal line just before the ball arrives. The ball hits their hands and drops to the ground. The first rule when catching the ball is that you must keep your eyes on the ball all the way in.

Second, when I'm drilling footballs at my receivers, I'm firmly admonishing them to watch the ball all the way into their hands. They nod in agreement, but their mind sometimes wanders. Perhaps they're thinking about the professor that gave them a bad grade, an argument with a girlfriend, or Coach Brown and "these stupid drills." Then the ball plops off their hands. They are seeing the ball, but the ball must be their only priority.

Then the third reason for dropping the pass is fear. In the 1988 UCLA game, our little 160-pound wingback, Dana Brinson, was reaching high for a pass. Just as the ball arrived, so did the UCLA defensive back with a devastating blow that knocked Dana on his back, hard. The first thought that came to my mind after he was pronounced okay was, will he ever come across the middle again to stretch out for a ball? So many times when a receiver gets hit like that, the next time he's wide open and the ball is coming to him, he will start to stretch for the ball, but then realize the last time he stretched out like this he got whacked pretty hard. All of a sudden those long arms God gave him to reach out and make great catches become like alligator arms. He begins to bend his elbows and not stretch out with great determination because of fear. Hence, the ball skims off of his hands.

The way I see it, God was like the quarterback in my life for the first 22 years. He had a ball in his hand in the form of His Son, Jesus Christ. For those 22 years, He kept throwing me passes. And for the same reasons receivers drop the ball, I was dropping God's ball, rejecting Christ. I had my eyes on this world and all the applause and the goals that people had set for me defining success, and I was rejecting Christ.

When I went to college, people encouraged me to go to church and join a Bible study. And every now and then out of a pang of guilt, I would show up maybe to gain a few points with God. But as I sat there I would get restless. My priority was not on Jesus Christ. I couldn't wait to get out. My mind would wander. I was rejecting Christ, dropping the ball. Finally, there was fear. I was afraid of becoming a Christian. I was afraid of what my friends would think. I was afraid if I ever became sold out for Jesus Christ perhaps He would take fun things like football out of my life and make me a missionary in Iceland or something like that.

God gave me some "receiver coaches" along the way. They weren't the answer for me, but they were people that helped point me in the right direction. They helped me to realize that there was something much greater than football, academic, or social success, something greater than success as the world would define it. Those things couldn't fulfill me. These "receiver coaches" helped point me in a direction so I could finally see the ball that God was throwing to me in the form of His son Jesus Christ. I finally made the greatest catch of my life on that day in 1979.

As you opened this book, perhaps you were thinking you wanted to find out more about your favorite player or coach. But little did you know God was sending you on a pass pattern. And now the ball is coming at you. If you have never made that great catch in your life, the gospel of Jesus Christ has been explained in this book. Are you going to continue to drop the ball?

I tell the receivers at Nebraska, if you keep dropping the ball, guess what? We will stop throwing it to you. We will throw to someone else who will catch it.

You don't know when the final pass will come to you. None of us are promised tomorrow. I encourage you that if you have never trusted Jesus Christ as your Savior and Lord to reach out and make that great catch. Only He can make you a champion in life. Only He can fulfill your every dream and every need.

For those of you who have made that great catch, one of the other things I tell the receivers at Nebraska, after making the catch, is to run with the ball. Get another yard. Try to score on every play.

What happens so often after we've made that great catch, after we've trusted Christ as our Savior and Lord, is we limp to the sideline of life, beaten, worn down, afraid. We cry and say it's too hard to play in the Christian game of life. They tackle us for our faith. They call us names. They spit at us. They persecute us. We sit down on the bench, head in the towel, crying, saying "I can't do it." And then Jesus Christ, the great coach on the sideline says, "Son, daughter, get back in the game. There are no bench warmers on my team. Everybody is a starting player. Everybody has a unique role in this game. And I've got a great plan for your life."

Some people are quarterbacks, in everything they do they receive glory. Some are offensive linemen. They get very little credit for what they do, but they open up holes for others to score. God has called each person in this world to a special role to make a tremendous contribution for Him, if they only give their lives to Him and allow Him to be their coach in every area of life. I encourage you to run with the ball. Go get another yard for God. When Cory Schlesinger dove into the end zone for the game-winning touchdown in the 1995 Orange Bowl national championship game, the officials raised both arms straight up in the air. Every Husker player, coach, and fan also raised their arms in exultation! One day, God will be standing on the "goal line" signaling "Touchdown, Touchdown, Touchdown!" As each Christian scores, I can't wait to be in the "Heavenly End Zone" that day. I hope that you will join the team–God's Team!